The Armored Fist

This volume is part of the Time-Life Books series,
THE NEW FACE OF WAR.
For information or to order the series,
please call 1-800-621-7026
(M-F 9am-6pm)
or write: Time-Life Customer Service
P.O. Box C32068
Richmond, Virginia 23261-2068

Other Publications:

HOW THINGS WORK
WINGS OF WAR
CREATIVE EVERYDAY COOKING
COLLECTOR'S LIBRARY OF THE UNKNOWN
CLASSICS OF WORLD WAR II
TIME-LIFE LIBRARY OF CURIOUS AND UNUSUAL FACTS
AMERICAN COUNTRY
VOYAGE THROUGH THE UNIVERSE
THE THIRD REICH
THE TIME-LIFE GARDENER'S GUIDE
MYSTERIES OF THE UNKNOWN
TIME FRAME
FIX IT YOURSELF
FITNESS, HEALTH & NUTRITION
SUCCESSFUL PARENTING
HEALTHY HOME COOKING
UNDERSTANDING COMPUTERS
LIBRARY OF NATIONS
THE ENCHANTED WORLD
THE KODAK LIBRARY OF CREATIVE PHOTOGRAPHY
GREAT MEALS IN MINUTES
THE CIVIL WAR
PLANET EARTH
COLLECTOR'S LIBRARY OF THE CIVIL WAR
THE EPIC OF FLIGHT
THE GOOD COOK
WORLD WAR II
HOME REPAIR AND IMPROVEMENT
THE OLD WEST

For information on and a full description of any
of the Time-Life Books series listed above,
please call 1-800-621-7026 or write:
Reader Information
Time-Life Customer Service
P.O. Box C-32068
Richmond, Virginia 23261-2068

THE NEW FACE OF WAR

The Armored Fist

BY THE EDITORS OF
TIME-LIFE BOOKS, ALEXANDRIA, VIRGINIA

CONSULTANTS

WILLIAM F. ATWATER, a former officer in the U.S. Marine Corps, is director of the U.S. Army Ordnance Museum at Aberdeen Proving Ground, Maryland.

RICHARD P. HUNNICUTT, a metallurgical engineer, is executive vice president of Anamet Laboratories in Hayward, California. He has written five books about armored vehicle development, including a comprehensive volume on the M1 Abrams main battle tank.

RON LEWANDOWSKI works for Honeywell Inc. in Minneapolis as project engineer for the Military Avionics Division. He has been involved in the development of advanced helmet display and helmet tracker systems at Honeywell for the past twenty years.

VINCENT MARCHESE manages the Sense And Destroy Armor (SADARM) project at the U.S. Army Armament Research, Development and Engineering Center at Picatinny Arsenal, New Jersey. He has been involved with the development of smart munitions since 1980.

PHILIP A. MOONEY was a lieutenant colonel in the U.S. Air Force and now manages Apache business development for McDonnell Douglas Helicopter Company in Mesa, Arizona. His twenty-year military career included two combat tours flying armed helicopters in Vietnam.

ROD PASCHALL, a former commander of Delta Force, was director of the U.S. Army Military History Institute at Carlisle Barracks, Pennsylvania. Now retired, he writes on many aspects of modern warfare, including low-intensity conflict, security affairs, and special operations.

DONN A. STARRY served in tank and cavalry units of the U.S. Army for more than thirty-five years before retiring as a four-star general. During the critical rebuilding years after the Vietnam War, he was the driving force behind much of Army doctrinal, equipment, organizational, and training development, especially for the Army's heavy forces.

VINCENT VINCI directs public relations and market development for Rockwell International's Tactical Systems Division in Duluth, Georgia. Author of numerous articles on aerospace, he has more than thirty years' experience in the fields of aerospace and defense.

CONTENTS

The Behemoths of Land War

Spitting fiery streaks of death from their machine guns (*above*), hurling bolts of destruction from their main guns, crushing obstacles beneath their treads, shrugging off storms of counterfire, tanks have rumbled through the twentieth century like beasts from another age. On land, they are the supreme threat, a tool of war whose speed, firepower, and steel-clad massiveness can hurt in many ways—by punching into rear areas and

over a dug-in enemy, by moving swiftly to cut off an
avenue of retreat, or simply by spreading a morale-sapping
chill of dread.

Tanks do not fight alone: Ordinarily, they are accompanied by lightly armored fighting vehicles, infantry carriers, helicopter gunships, engineers, mobile artillery, and
other complementary forces. Nor do they thrive everywhere. As pictured here, M48 Patton tanks and M113 armored cavalry assault vehicles could be formidable

in sweep operations in Vietnam, but their scope was limited: Much of the country's jungled terrain deterred armor.
In the bloody territorial struggle fought by Iraq and Iran
from 1980 to 1988, armor was sometimes thwarted by a
marshy battle zone. Nonetheless, the tank and its deadly
retinue have remained at the center of modern land warfare, demonstrating their primacy in arenas ranging from
the deserts of the Middle East to the urban battlefields of
Bucharest and Beijing.

On th[...]
Syria, [...]
Israeli M[...]
krieg tact[...]
with devas[...]
Germans in [...] blitz-
krieg—mean[...] ightning
war"—calls for slashing, oppor-
tunistic attacks by fast-moving
columns of armor. In the 1967
war, Israeli forces—greatly outnumbered but better trained
and far more mobile than the
opposition—cut through and
around enemy positions to
win an overwhelming victory
in just six days.

Dug in for protection against the antitank weapons of Afghan rebels, a Soviet T-62 guards the route between the cities of Kabul and Jalālābād in 1980. The Soviets mostly used tanks in such defensive roles during their ten-year effort to suppress the Mujahedin (freedom fighters) of Afghanistan. When tanks ventured forth on the country's narrow mountain roads, they often fell victim to mines, antitank rockets, and rebel-launched landslides.

At the climax of the revolution that brought down Romanian dictator Nicolai Ceausescu in December 1989, Army tanks roll into Bucharest's Palace Square, a scene of intense fighting against the Securitate—the regime's heavily armed, 180,000-man secret police. In the inset picture, soldiers and citizens take cover behind a tank as one of its crew swings his machine gun toward a Securitate sniper.

With no weapon but his own outrage against oppression, a lone citizen halts a column of tanks sent into Beijing in June 1989 to overawe antigovernment protesters occupying Tiananmen Square, the capital's symbolic center. The standoff of student-led demonstrators and China's rulers lasted seven weeks. In the end, steel proved stronger than words. Tanks roared through the square, crushing students caught in the open and churning over tents with people still inside.

1

A Juggernaut of Men and Machines

Roaring over the dunes of the Saudi Arabian desert, a platoon of M1A1 tanks from the 24th Mechanized Infantry Division takes part in an exercise in connection with Operation Desert Shield. A command tank *(foreground)* can be recognized by its two radio antennas. The one on the left, which every tank has, permits communication between tanks. The antenna on the right is used to call in air strikes.

Thousands of stars illuminate the moonless Arabian night. Rehearsal is about to begin. The lieutenant commanding an American tank platoon stands in the hatch of his sixty-three-ton M1 Abrams main battle tank surveying the scene with night-vision goggles. Through the lingering, talc-fine dust raised as his outfit moved into position on the line of departure, he can see the green luminescent images of the three other tanks in his charge spaced 100 yards apart in a combat wedge echeloned to the right. Not far behind him stands a supporting platoon of four twenty-two-ton M2 Bradley fighting vehicles, each bristling with machine guns and a rapid-firing 25-mm cannon. Inside rides a crew of three and eight heavily armed infantrymen. Farther back, other Bradleys are armed with a pair of wire-guided TOW antitank missile launchers.

Engines are running. As the second hand on the platoon leader's watch sweeps toward two in the morning—H-hour—a green flare arcs into the sky, fired by the company commander standing in the hatch of his Bradley command vehicle some distance away. The lieutenant speaks into the intercom: "Operation Sandstorm, now," instructing his driver to advance. The platoon accelerates in a whoosh of gas-turbine engines to a speed of about forty miles per hour. The whiny growl of diesels crescendos as the Bradleys move out behind them. Several miles ahead, just beyond the horizon, lie mock defensive positions like those of the Iraqi Army.

To the right, left, and rear churn more Abrams with their supporting Bradleys and other vehicles—three tank platoons to a company, four companies to a battalion, between three and five battalions to a maneuver brigade, three brigades to a division. Tonight, two battalions, one of armor and one of mechanized infantry, are in action, concentrated on a front only 500 yards wide: fifty-eight

Abrams, fifty-four Bradleys carrying infantry, a dozen Bradley derivatives called cavalry fighting vehicles, twelve specialized tracked vehicles armed with TOWs, and six towed 107-mm mortars.

As the desert comes alive with charging armor, helicopters launched in radio silence from bases in the rear overtake the MBTs and Bradleys and precede them toward the point of attack. In the lead are half a dozen lightly armed Kiowa scouts. Their assignment is to scoot toward the mocked-up line of enemy strongpoints, searching out targets for heavily armed Apache attack helicopters that follow. Tank busters of the first order, the Apaches are to take on enemy armor reserves with Hellfire laser-guided missiles or work over defensive positions with rockets and 30-mm cannon to take as much fight out of the enemy as possible before the American tanks and infantry arrive.

Before dawn, this exercise is over. The Abrams and Bradleys trundle back to their night defensive positions dug into the desert some fifty miles south of the Kuwaiti border. Postmortem after breakfast.

Such were the sights and sounds of the desert in the autumn of 1990, as the U.S. 24th Mechanized Infantry Division practiced coordinating the rush of armor as it would descend on Iraqi invaders of Kuwait in the event they moved against Saudi Arabia—or if the Americans and their allies should be ordered to expel them from the country they had ravaged the preceding summer and now occupied with 500,000 troops and more.

The 24th is arguably the most potent single armor division ever assembled: 17,000 men, 348 Abrams, 208 Bradleys, 144 launchers for Dragon light antitank missiles, another 4,500 tracked and wheeled vehicles, plus 150 helicopters of various types. The division's deployment—indeed, the entire United Nations effort—would go down as one of military history's supreme feats of logistics, involving a hitherto unprecedented airlift and sealift. Within two days of an alert issued to the division's Fort Stewart, Georgia, headquarters on August 8, the first of the 24th's combat and support troops would be winging their way 8,000 air miles to Dhahran, Saudi Arabia, in a fleet of civilian airliners. In the meantime, their equipment was being loaded onto a flotilla of enormous U.S. Navy armor transports, ships capable of thirty-three knots burdened with hundreds of MBTs, fighting vehicles, trucks, and artillery pieces—

plus ammunition, fuel, food, and other supplies. Despite mishaps that delayed two of the vessels, the first of the 24th's weaponry would reach the waiting troops in Saudi Arabia nineteen days and 12,000 sea miles later.

If it came to war, the 24th Division's 348 Abrams would be joined by perhaps another 3,500 modern main battle tanks—2,500 in other U.S. Army and Marine units, 1,000 more from allied forces. The Iraqis might counter with as many as 5,500 MBTs of various descriptions, mostly Soviet-made and in varying levels of technology and states of repair. Yet even Iraq's immense weight of armor would amount to only a paltry fraction—roughly three percent—of the 170,000 or so main battle tanks in the world's armies. Including light tanks, infantry fighting vehicles, and armored personnel carriers, the total armored inventory exceeds a monumental 300,000 units. Before the end of the Cold War, the Soviet Union and its Warsaw Pact allies together boasted nearly 160,000 armored vehicles, including 78,000 MBTs; the United States and NATO, opting for quality over quantity, manned more than 34,000 MBTs and 61,000 other armored vehicles.

The governments of the Middle East and North Africa control no fewer than 23,000 main battle tanks, with Syria (4,050), Israel (3,794), Egypt (2,425), and Libya (1,800) being the most heavily armored after Iraq. Meanwhile, China and the other nations of Asia field yet another 23,000 MBTs. At the low end of the scale, the lands of sub-Saharan Africa and Latin America nevertheless count more than 4,000 main battle tanks among them. And it is the rare nation that does not regard some sort of armor as essential to its security. Togo, a tiny country on Africa's Atlantic coast, takes comfort in a pair of MBTs (plus nine light tanks). Even Luxembourg has four armored personnel carriers among its minuscule armed forces.

For it is axiomatic in modern affairs that any severe or prolonged confrontation will sooner or later see the appearance of armor—if only to guard a strike-torn factory or cow an unruly mob. Yet for all its versatility, the tank is best at fighting other tanks in a battle of maneuver, breakthrough, and encirclement. That is the mission of the 24th Mechanized and other allied armor in Saudi Arabia—if need be, to concentrate overwhelming mobile firepower against the opponent; to use tanks and infantry to defeat his armor and reduce his strongpoints; and to smash through, envelop, and destroy his remaining defenses.

Heinz Guderian, master armor tactician of the Third Reich's Wehrmacht, introduced this kind of fighting in World War II. The Germans called it *Blitzkrieg.* "It has been said," argued Guderian, "that only movement brings victory," and in raising the German Army from the ashes of the First World War, Guderian sought to reverse the notion that tanks should fight in support of infantry and travel at the foot soldier's speed. Instead, he saw tanks as the Army's principal weapon, moving swiftly to apply decisive firepower against an enemy line, with fully motorized infantry and artillery following close in support. The key to the tactic was the *Schwerpunkt.* German for "point of concentration," the word expressed Guderian's concept of massing forces to break through enemy defenses at one or perhaps two points, then strike rapidly into lightly defended rear areas.

A ferocious debate arose between Guderian and his fellow generals, and though he did not win every point, he prevailed to build a combined-arms Panzer Corps that ran rampant in the early days of the war. In the 1940 assault on France, Guderian's XIX Corps drove 149 miles to the Channel coast in scarcely seven days. A year later, launching Operation Barbarossa against the Soviet Union, his Panzer Group Two slashed an astonishing 273 miles through enemy defenses in the course of the first week, arriving at Smolensk—413 miles east of the Polish border—within a fortnight. Before the German panzers were finally halted within sight of Moscow, they had accomplished no fewer than twenty-two encirclements, had captured more than 14,000 tanks and 25,000 guns, and had taken almost three million Soviet prisoners. When the tide

Colonel-General Heinz Guderian, pioneer of the combined-arms theory of warfare, was the architect of some of Germany's most spectacular victories early in World War II. But when the Russians counterattacked outside Moscow in the winter of 1941, he was sacked for daring to disagree with Hitler's "not one step backward" policy. Such folly was anathema to Guderian's concept of a mobile armored reserve as the best form of defense.

turned in 1943, panzers, dug into hull-down positions along the lines of access and backed by mobile reserves, provided the German Army's most effective defense against the Soviet juggernaut.

Transplanted to the short, vicious conflicts in the Middle East during the 1960s and 1970s, Guderian's insights into the offensive and defensive application of armor have proved to be more enduring—and immutable—than even he might have imagined. In the Six-Day War against Egypt and Syria in 1967, Israeli tanks seemed to be invincible, leading the Army to question whether Guderian's insistence on supporting infantry still applied. Deciding that it did not, the Israeli Armored Corps sought to change the rules. Six years later, in the Yom Kippur War, Israeli tank formations charged ahead without infantry support only to be bloodied by Egyptian tanks backed by a host of missile-firing Egyptian foot soldiers. Only when Israeli tank commanders relented and took the infantry with them would they defeat the Egyptians. A similar validation of combined arms—this time in defense—would occur to the north against Syria on the rocky Golan Heights, where cleverly dug-in Israeli armor backed by a mobile reserve would hold off an assault by vastly greater numbers of Syrian tanks.

Such bloody battlefields would serve as laboratories for equipment as well as tactics. From lessons learned there would evolve new generations of main battle tanks far bigger, quicker, and more nimble than ever before. Some would be powered by aircraft-style turbines instead of reciprocating engines. Most would be armed with massive smoothbore cannons firing hypervelocity rounds of unprecedented penetrating power. And all would wear suits of complex armor designed to defeat those munitions. Technological innovations would allow tanks not only to fire accurately under circumstances in which scoring would have been pure luck for their forerunners, but also to radically improve the crew's chances for survival in case of a hit.

Such state-of-the-art technology was expected to give the United States and its allies the edge over numerically superior Iraqi armor in any shooting war. "We were out there doing maneuvers the other day," said the sergeant gunner of an Abrams M1. "We were moving along at a pretty good clip, and at 1,200 yards I was able to keep my sights right on another tank with hardly any movement at all. That's our advantage over them—fire and maneuver. That and our nighttime capability."

☆

2

October 1973: Melee in the Desert

Columns of smoke on the horizon mark a bombing attack on the Suez front as seen over the 105-mm main gun of an Israeli tank. The open, sandy terrain east of the Suez Canal in the Sinai Peninsula was the arena for some of the most ferocious armored combat in history.

Israel started October 6, 1973, with prayer and fasting. That day was Yom Kippur, the Day of Atonement, holiest of all occasions in the Jewish calendar. But this year's observance would be different. To the shock of the entire nation, its people would begin dying in war before the sun went down.

Some of the first casualties were among the 600 Israeli soldiers manning the Bar-Lev Line, a chain of bunkers guarding the east bank of the 110-mile-long Suez Canal, which separated the Israeli-held Sinai Peninsula from Egypt. This defensive network—built after the capture of the Sinai from Egypt in the Six-Day War of 1967 and named for the guiding force behind its construction, General Haim Bar-Lev—was a frail wall, its sixteen strongpoints spaced miles apart, its garrison seriously understrength.

Still, there seemed no great reason for worry. About 270 tanks were deployed ten to fifteen miles back from the bunkers, ready to race forward to meet any Egyptian thrust. The Canal itself was an imposing barrier—"one of the best antitank ditches available," said Minister of Defense Moshe Dayan. And apart from the particulars of defense, the Israelis simply had little respect for the fighting abilities of the Arabs. After four wars fought against its neighbors since 1948, the little nation felt supremely confident that it would prevail in battle, no matter how ardently its enemies wanted their lost territories back.

That confidence was now about to be put to the test. At two o'clock in the afternoon, 2,000 Egyptian artillery pieces and heavy mortars unleashed a furious barrage against the Bar-Lev Line. At the same time, more than 200 Soviet-supplied MiGs and Sukhoi fighter-bombers raced across the Suez Canal to attack Israeli supply depots, command centers, and forward airfields in the Sinai, and Egyptian commandos, transported by helicopter, set up ambush sites along the main access roads from Israel to the Suez front. It was a devastating blow—and it was not the only one that was to fall at that hour.

Egypt's President Anwar Sadat had made his war plans in league with President Hafez Assad of Syria, who, no less than Sadat, was determined to recover land his country had lost in 1967. Thus, even as guns thundered along the Suez, war burst upon the northeastern border of Israel with stunning force. Six hundred Syrian artillery pieces opened fire as 1,200 Soviet-made tanks surged toward an Israeli force defending the Golan Heights—a seventeen-mile-deep stretch of desolate volcanic terrain that rises steeply from the Jordan River valley and slopes away toward the Syrian plain. Only 176 tanks, along with a sprinkling of infantry in armored personnel carriers, and self-propelled artillery, stood between the Syrians and the settlements of northern Israel.

The most furious tank warfare since World War II lay ahead. It would validate some tenets of tank combat dating back to the German blitzkrieg into Poland—the use of fast-moving, air-supported armor and mechanized infantry to slash through enemy defenses. At the same time, it would demonstrate—in a shocking way—the potency of new antitank weapons.

When the artillery barrage on the Suez front slackened after twenty minutes, the first wave of an Egyptian infantry force numbering 8,000 troops scrambled down to the water at twenty points along the entire length of the Canal. Rubber assault boats carried the soldiers across its 200-yard width in minutes. Using ropes and ladders, they scrambled up the high earthen ramparts built along the east bank of the Canal, bypassed the Bar-Lev strongpoints, and

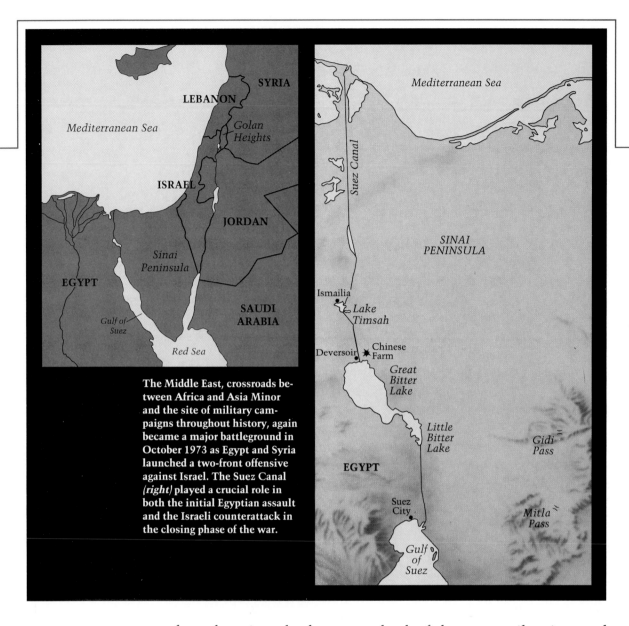

The Middle East, crossroads between Africa and Asia Minor and the site of military campaigns throughout history, again became a major battleground in October 1973 as Egypt and Syria launched a two-front offensive against Israel. The Suez Canal *(right)* played a crucial role in both the initial Egyptian assault and the Israeli counterattack in the closing phase of the war.

fanned out into the desert to a depth of about two miles. A second wave followed and launched an assault on the Bar-Lev bunkers themselves. At the same time, portable antiaircraft missiles—Soviet-built SA-7s—were deployed to stave off Israeli warplanes, and an armored brigade equipped with Soviet PT-76 amphibious tanks churned across the Great Bitter Lake, which forms part of the Canal. That night, engineers would bridge the Canal to bring heavier armor into the Sinai. In good part because months had been spent on careful planning and rehearsal, the operation appeared to be succeeding beyond the wildest Egyptian hopes. Instead of costing thousands of lives, as Sadat's generals had feared, the crossing claimed the lives of only 208.

Israeli soldiers pinned in their bunkers noticed that many of the Egyptian infantrymen lugged unusual packs that looked like canvas-covered suitcases. Upon reaching the perimeter of the bridgehead, the infantry opened these cases to reveal a new weapon of Soviet manufacture known to the West as the Sagger antitank guided missile. Other soldiers carried tubes with a cone-shaped device at one end. These proved to be rocket-propelled grenades (RPGs), upgraded versions of the World War II bazooka. Both weapons would find immediate use.

The onset of war had not taken the Israeli high command completely by surprise. On both the Suez and Golan fronts, the marshaling of Arab forces had been apparent, and two days earlier, Israeli intelligence had detected the families of Soviet military advisers leaving both Egypt and Syria—a sign of imminent hostilities. But because of previous false alarms and the disruption to the economy of mobilizing its citizen army of reserves, the country's leaders decided against such a move until the last possible minute.

Yuval Neria was a lieutenant in the regular army and deputy commander of a tank company in the armored force deployed behind the Bar-Lev Line. When his unit learned that the Egyptians had crossed the Canal, it set off for its assigned station in the northern sector of the front. On the radio net that linked him to the bunkers of the Bar-Lev Line—many of them already cut off and surrounded—Neria heard a voice say, "The catastrophe has begun."

When his tanks approached the Canal, they were greeted by a fusillade of Saggers. Crude predecessors of the Sagger had been seen by some Israeli tankers in skirmishes that had occurred between 1967 and 1970. But the Saggers were faster and more accurate, and there seems to have been no concerted effort to prepare the Israeli Armored Corps for what would prove to be the greatest innovation in weapons technology of that war. "We were never told to expect and didn't train against missiles," says one Israeli officer. And a sergeant adds, "I was an instructor in the armor school just before the war and we never taught how to cope with missiles and infantry to any extent."

Two-man teams readied the Sagger's self-contained launcher and fired the missile; one member of the team then guided it to the target with a simple optical sight and a joystick that sent electrical signals down hair-fine wires unreeling behind the missile. Skimming over the ground with flame blossoming from its exhaust, it took about fifteen seconds to travel its effective range of about a mile. Abdul Alati, in charge of an Egyptian antitank missile detachment, claimed eight Israeli tanks destroyed in ten minutes

An Egyptian T-55 kicks up a cloud of sand as it speeds to the front. Thick armor, a low profile, and a 100-mm rifled main gun made this tank a formidable adversary. Far outnumbering the more modern T-62, it was the mainstay of the Arab armored divisions in the October War.

with this weapon. "The tanks accelerated to their maximum speed to avoid our rockets," he recalled, "but we could hit them in their weakest spots as long as they remained in range. Every Egyptian missile was worth an Israeli tank."

This was an exaggeration, but the Israelis quickly learned to respect the Saggers. Neria later described his initiation: "It was a muddy area, a marsh. The people reacting to the missiles were trying to maneuver, trying to escape them, to confuse the missile launchers by zigzagging." They had no chance. "Half an hour after we arrived in the area, we were more or less finished as a company." Neria had started with eleven tanks; now only his tank and one other were still operational.

Comparable losses were occurring all along the Bar-Lev Line as Israeli tanks tried to relieve the besieged bunkers and deny Egyptian engineers any opportunity to bridge the Canal. Missiles and rocket-propelled grenades were not the only threat. Egyptian tanks positioned on sand ramps along the Canal's opposite bank fired down on the Israelis. As Moshe Dayan admitted later, "Our effort to bring up tanks to the Canal to prevent the erection of a bridge cost us very dear. We hadn't anticipated that."

Nor did the Israelis foresee the resourcefulness of the Egyptian engineers. As the missile infantry fended off tanks and aircraft with their Saggers, RPGs, and surface-to-air missiles, the bridge builders went to work with a fury, aiming to get the needed mass of tanks and heavy weapons across within twenty-four hours. Through the night of October 6, they pieced together ten sectional pontoon bridges. But the water divide was only part of their problem. The way was also blocked by the earthen dike along the east bank of the Canal, twenty to thirty feet high in most places, and raised to a height of seventy-five feet by the Israelis at critical points. For tanks to get past the barrier, the Egyptians would have to make numerous twenty-foot-wide holes through it, each requiring the removal of about 1,500 cubic yards of sand and earth.

The original plan had been to excavate openings with dynamite or even heavy guns. Then, as Chief of Staff Saad el Shazli remem-

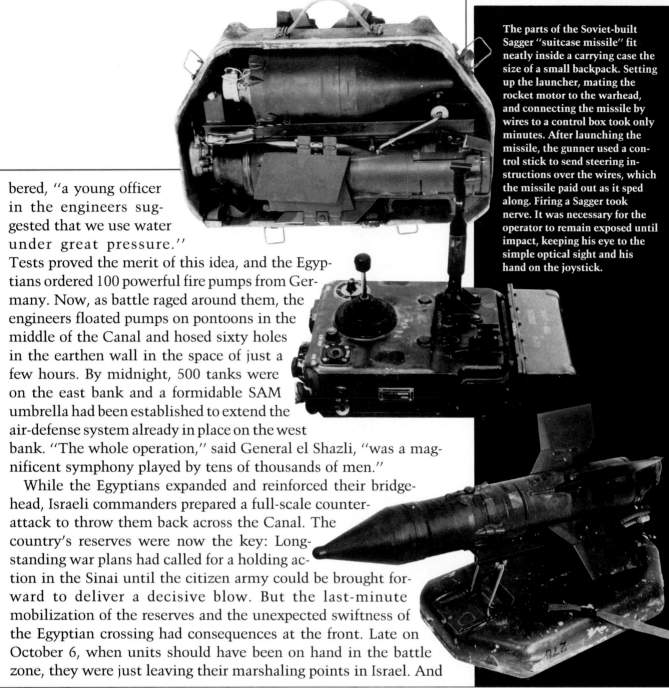

bered, "a young officer in the engineers suggested that we use water under great pressure." Tests proved the merit of this idea, and the Egyptians ordered 100 powerful fire pumps from Germany. Now, as battle raged around them, the engineers floated pumps on pontoons in the middle of the Canal and hosed sixty holes in the earthen wall in the space of just a few hours. By midnight, 500 tanks were on the east bank and a formidable SAM umbrella had been established to extend the air-defense system already in place on the west bank. "The whole operation," said General el Shazli, "was a magnificent symphony played by tens of thousands of men."

While the Egyptians expanded and reinforced their bridgehead, Israeli commanders prepared a full-scale counterattack to throw them back across the Canal. The country's reserves were now the key: Long-standing war plans had called for a holding action in the Sinai until the citizen army could be brought forward to deliver a decisive blow. But the last-minute mobilization of the reserves and the unexpected swiftness of the Egyptian crossing had consequences at the front. Late on October 6, when units should have been on hand in the battle zone, they were just leaving their marshaling points in Israel. And

upon arriving at their supply depots, the reservists frequently discovered that equipment and war stocks were lacking. Captain David Halevy, company commander in an armored reconnaissance battalion, later remembered that his unit "went to war without binoculars, without one map, without enough ammunition."

Nor had Halevy and his comrades prepared for the type of war they would fight. Like Israel's high command, they were overconfident. Halevy candidly admitted, "You have to keep in mind that we were ordinary Israelis who believed in our own legend and the legend was we are unbeatable." In 1967, the Armored Corps had fought a fast-moving offensive war, sweeping across the breadth of the Sinai in a few days and sowing confusion and panic among the Egyptians by appearing where they were least expected. Infantry had played a minimal role, as tank crews traded support from foot soldiers for bold thrusts into the enemy's territory that seemed to echo the sorties of fighter-bombers overhead. Israel's astounding success in the Six-Day War had convinced the Armored Corps that tanks were unstoppable—and that anything likely to retard their advance, such as infantry in their thin-skinned armored personnel carriers (APCs), should be left behind. But in that war, a mere six years earlier, there had been no hordes of dug-in tank-killer teams to contend with.

Now, on the morning of October 8, the first wave of reserves rushing across the desert from Israel joined with the remains of the standing armored force in the Sinai and went on the offensive. The result was calamitous.

Major Chaim Adini, commander of an Israeli tank battalion that took part in the battle, was ordered to advance on the Egyptian bridge at Firdan near the center of the front and capture it. "My first question was 'Do I have any artillery?' The answer was 'Yes, you will have it.' 'Do I have air support?' The answer was 'Yes, of course.' I asked again and the answer was 'Chaim, you will have all the support you need. Move.' "

He and his men were confident of quick victory as they headed for the bridge, which lay a couple of miles to the west across flat and open terrain, perfect tank country. His twenty-two-tank battalion was arrayed in a three-pronged formation: two companies in front for mutual fire support and one behind as a reserve—"according to the book," said Adini. They spotted some Egyptian tanks beside the Canal and destroyed them at long range. Then the desert ahead

When attacking, tank units try to reconcile two conflicting demands—to fire at the enemy ahead without leaving their vulnerable flanks unprotected. To this end, tactical formations have been devised that are remarkably similar in armies everywhere.

As shown on these pages, there are five basic tank formations. All of them are organized around the tank platoon, a unit that consists of three to five vehicles and is the basic strike force of armored warfare. The same formations are used in various combinations when platoons assemble into companies, battalions, and brigades for a major assault *(page 32)*.

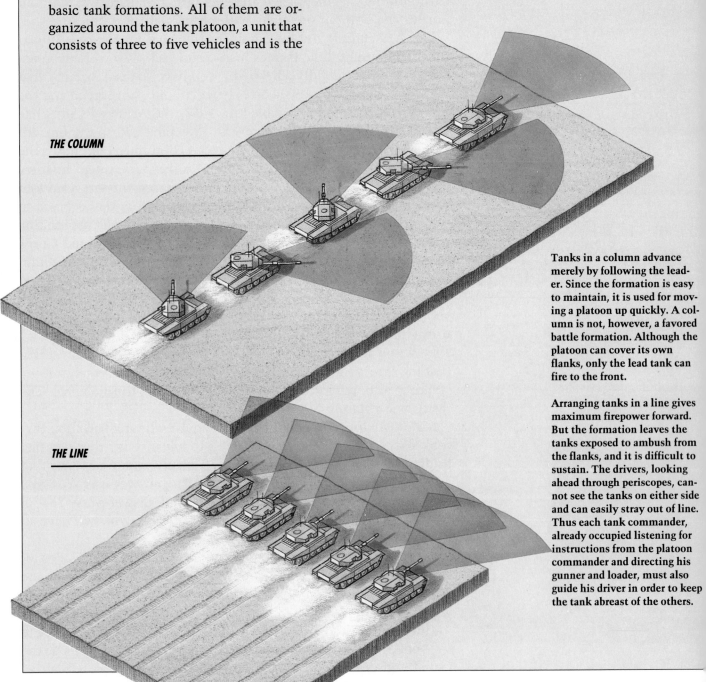

THE COLUMN

Tanks in a column advance merely by following the leader. Since the formation is easy to maintain, it is used for moving a platoon up quickly. A column is not, however, a favored battle formation. Although the platoon can cover its own flanks, only the lead tank can fire to the front.

THE LINE

Arranging tanks in a line gives maximum firepower forward. But the formation leaves the tanks exposed to ambush from the flanks, and it is difficult to sustain. The drivers, looking ahead through periscopes, cannot see the tanks on either side and can easily stray out of line. Thus each tank commander, already occupied listening for instructions from the platoon commander and directing his gunner and loader, must also guide his driver in order to keep the tank abreast of the others.

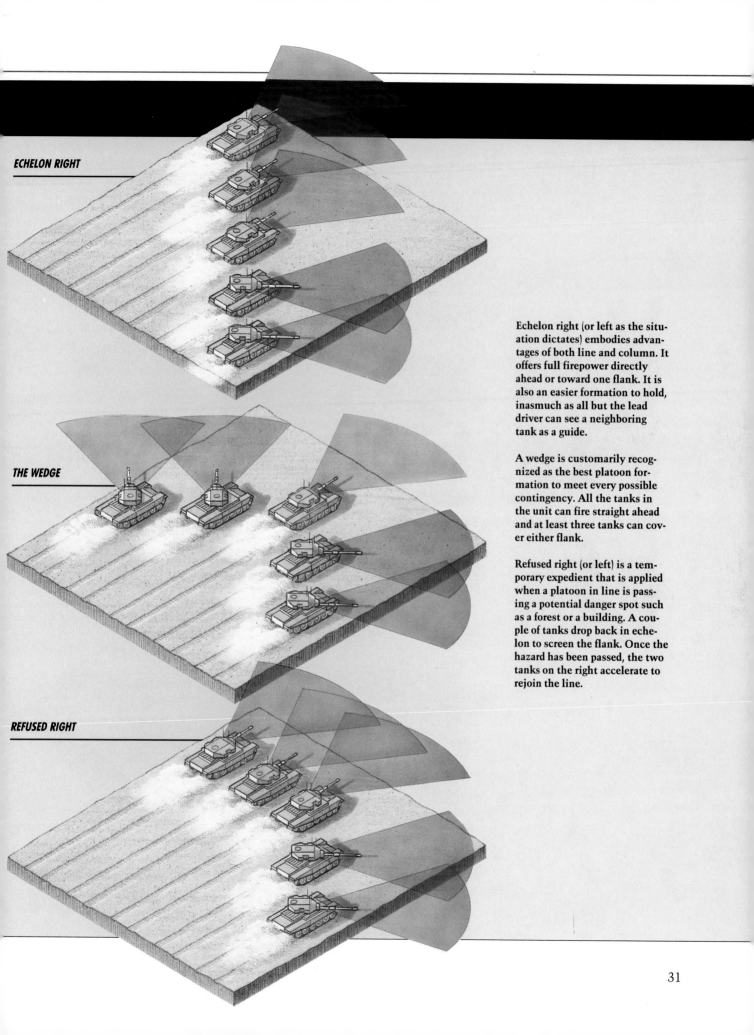

ECHELON RIGHT

THE WEDGE

REFUSED RIGHT

Echelon right (or left as the situation dictates) embodies advantages of both line and column. It offers full firepower directly ahead or toward one flank. It is also an easier formation to hold, inasmuch as all but the lead driver can see a neighboring tank as a guide.

A wedge is customarily recognized as the best platoon formation to meet every possible contingency. All the tanks in the unit can fire straight ahead and at least three tanks can cover either flank.

Refused right (or left) is a temporary expedient that is applied when a platoon in line is passing a potential danger spot such as a forest or a building. A couple of tanks drop back in echelon to screen the flank. Once the hazard has been passed, the two tanks on the right accelerate to rejoin the line.

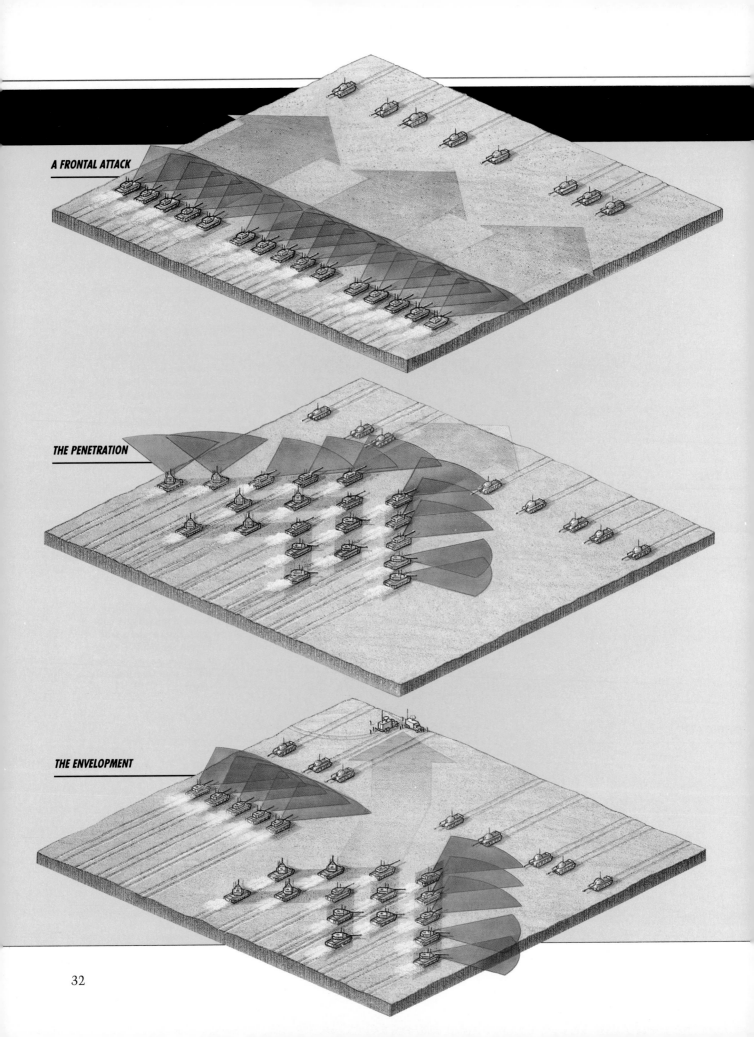

A FRONTAL ATTACK

THE PENETRATION

THE ENVELOPMENT

Tank platoons do battle according to the objective. Against a solid front, for example, they might attack in a line. A frontal assault of this kind is risky, since it spreads firepower over a broad area. Yet it can rout a weak enemy caught in the open without prepared defenses.

A penetration attack attempts a narrow breach of the enemy's defenses to attack the rear. The two platoons advancing in echelon crack the enemy line, then hold the gap open. Follow-on platoons, formed as wedges, race through the opening toward a distant objective.

Envelopment strikes the enemy rear along an unexpected axis. In the bottom drawing, a platoon on the left flank pins the enemy unit to its front while another platoon in echelon covers the right. Platoons formed as wedges push through the opening, then veer left to capture enemy command posts.

suddenly blazed with fire. "In front of us was a sea of Egyptian infantry with Saggers," Adini later recalled. "We were the only Israeli unit in that area at that time. It was supposed to be a major attack, not a battalion, not a brigade—the whole division." A swarm of missiles came at them. "I shouted into my microphone to the other tanks to go left, go right to avoid the Saggers." Within a minute, Adini lost four tanks.

Nonetheless, he pushed on for another half-mile, until he found himself in the midst of thousands of Egyptian infantrymen hidden in foxholes in the sand. "We used our machine guns and Uzis to save ourselves. We used our main gun at a distance of five meters." But a tank's 105-mm gun, designed to pierce armor at ranges up to 3,000 yards, was not much use against a solitary soldier in a foxhole less than twenty feet away. The soldier, however, possessed an antitank weapon ideally suited for that distance. "I remember one Egyptian," Adini said. "He was a very brave guy, he stood just in front of my tank with an RPG and fired. It struck my tank and struck me and I fell down into the tank." Adini at first thought he had been blinded; he could not see because his face was covered with blood. When he wiped the blood away, his vision returned. "It took me two or three minutes to recover. Then I stood up and started giving orders to the other tanks to go back. There was no artillery support, no air cover, no tanks behind me. I thought it was time to save my people." In this brief action, Adini had lost another five tanks to the RPGs and Saggers.

About four hours later, another tank battalion, commanded by Lieutenant Colonel Assaf Yagouri, launched a similar attack in the same area. Coordination among the Israeli units that day was so poor that Yagouri had not heard about the fate of Adini's battalion. Brigadier General Hassan Abu A'Saada, commander of the Egyptian troops in that sector of the bridgehead, later said, "Yagouri made tactical mistakes. Our troops and tanks were well dug in. Yagouri sent out ten tanks, and we destroyed seven. Then he sent out thirteen and we destroyed four." General A'Saada decided to allow the Israelis to penetrate his front line to a depth of five hundred yards. When Yagouri's main force charged at high speed, the Egyptians sprang a trap. "It was men against tanks," said A'Saada. "Frequently they were knocking out a tank from the rear after it had gone by. That takes courage and determination. The Israelis were wiped out in three minutes, having scarcely fired a shot." Yagouri's tank was disabled and fell into a gully. The unfortunate colonel was captured, his force decimated.

The Armored Corps's doctrine of tank-only units conducting cavalry-style charges suddenly seemed as outmoded as cavalry itself. But at least once on that chaotic third day of the war, the tanks were accompanied by infantry. Even so, the assault was weak and poorly coordinated. Captain David Halevy's reconnaissance unit, mounted in armored personnel carriers, participated. They were perched on the highest sand dune in the area north of Firdan, with an unobstructed view of the flat terrain between them and the Canal. About midmorning, he received instructions from his divisional headquarters to charge.

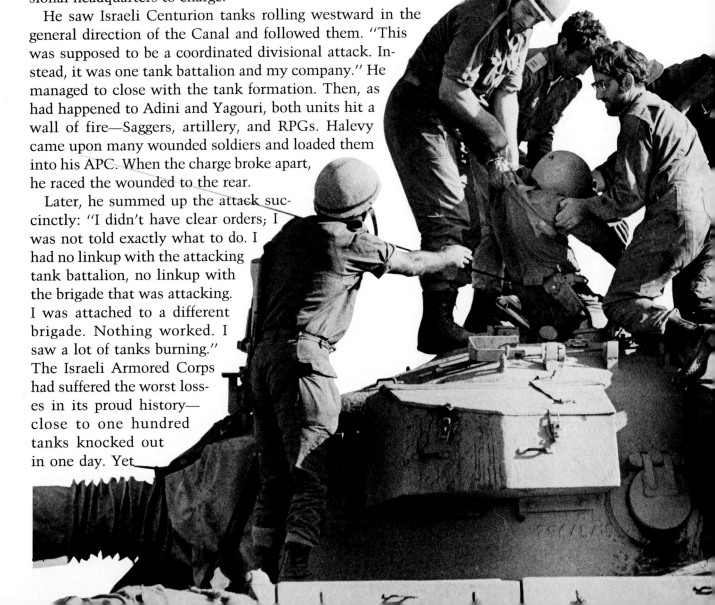

Medics and fellow tankers gently lift a wounded Israeli crewman from the turret of his Centurion tank. Straps attached to the back of tankers' overalls facilitate removal of casualties from the tight confines of their vehicles.

He saw Israeli Centurion tanks rolling westward in the general direction of the Canal and followed them. "This was supposed to be a coordinated divisional attack. Instead, it was one tank battalion and my company." He managed to close with the tank formation. Then, as had happened to Adini and Yagouri, both units hit a wall of fire—Saggers, artillery, and RPGs. Halevy came upon many wounded soldiers and loaded them into his APC. When the charge broke apart, he raced the wounded to the rear.

Later, he summed up the attack succinctly: "I didn't have clear orders; I was not told exactly what to do. I had no linkup with the attacking tank battalion, no linkup with the brigade that was attacking. I was attached to a different brigade. Nothing worked. I saw a lot of tanks burning." The Israeli Armored Corps had suffered the worst losses in its proud history— close to one hundred tanks knocked out in one day. Yet it had failed to make a dent in the Egyptian defensive perimeter.

After his ill-fated charge, Halevy returned to his observation post on the high dune and witnessed a sight he would never forget. "The radio was crackling, the division was talking about total disaster, failure on the battlefield." His unit alone seemed to be holding its position. Tanks were rolling eastward instead of westward. He saw some tanks stop; the hatches opened, and people jumped out and started running. "That was not the Israeli Army I knew," he said later. Since his battalion was a divisional reconnaissance unit, every vehicle and every soldier had access to the divisional radio net. "The divisional network was talking in the clear, no codes. The message was that we were losing, the division was melting." Halevy switched to his company's frequency and said to everybody listening, "I don't know what's going on, but we were told to hold this position and we'll hold it. No matter what the price, we'll hold it." The Egyptians, content with their success so far, did not press their advantage, and Halevy's men retained the hill.

Yuval Neria, who had been ambushed at the Bar-Lev Line on the war's first day, saw his share of action on October 8. His reduced company joined a battalion in another brigade. Taking position in an area of towering sand dunes south of Halevy's unit, they shot at Egyptian tanks all around them, hitting as many as twenty. Then, on orders from the battalion commander, Lieutenant Colonel Amir Yoffe, they rolled forward to occupy the crest of the dunes. As his tank started to climb a steep slope, Neria looked behind him from his vantage point in the open commander's hatch and saw an Egyptian tank about five hundred yards away. It opened fire, hitting Neria's tank in the rear engine compartment. "I felt the vibration under my feet. The tank stopped and I shouted to my crew to jump out." Neria remembered to grab his Uzi. "At the very moment we jumped, there was another explosion. The tank had taken another hit and caught fire." Miraculously, none of his crew was wounded. As they scrambled down the dune, the nearest Israeli troops, thinking they were Egyptians, began to fire at them. Neria waved the Uzi over his head, and the firing stopped. He and his crew made it back to their lines safely.

When Neria saw Yoffe an hour or so later, he asked him what had happened to his friends on the hill. Yoffe's tank was a wreck, the barrel of the main gun shattered. He was very depressed as he told Neria that only a few had come back. "It was hell," Neria says. "I was pretty sad. I spent the night on Yoffe's tank." During the first three days of the war, the Israeli Armored Corps had received a bloody education, and the futile assaults against the Egyptian bridgehead were not renewed after October 8. The dismissive attitude toward the enemy's ability was gone.

So far, the Egyptian military strategy had worked brilliantly. Commander in Chief Ahmed Ali Ismail had plotted the war as a swift succession of offense and defense: His forces would first strike across the Suez Canal, then stop, dig in, and protect the position with a massive array of weaponry. Any further action would depend on what the Israelis did. The Egyptian bridgehead was about ten miles deep—about half as deep as planned. But that was ten miles more than the Israelis had ever envisioned.

The Sinai front would remain mostly static for the next week. On the Israeli side, a drastic rethinking of tank tactics was called for. In the past, the Israelis had proved masters of adaptation, and now they began to see what was needed: Out with the new, in with the old. The Armored Corps would revert to a combined-arms doctrine that General Guderian would have instantly recognized.

A Duel of Armor in the North

When Israel's military leaders studied the Golan Heights as a potential battlefield, the contrast with the Sinai was dramatic. Its stony escarpment, punctuated with scrub vegetation and rock outcroppings, would hamper the enemy's off-road movement and channel armored formations into restricted avenues of attack. Captured from Syria in the Six-Day War, the Golan had natural defensive attributes that had been considerably strengthened by Israeli combat engineers. They constructed bunkers, minefields, fighting positions for tanks, and an antitank ditch eighteen feet deep and eighteen to twenty-five feet wide along the entire forty-mile length of the cease-fire boundary, known as the Purple Line. The Syrian Army lay to the east, on the far side of a broad, shallow valley, which, owing to the events of the next few days, would acquire a new sobriquet—the Valley of Tears.

At five minutes before two on the afternoon of October 6, Israeli

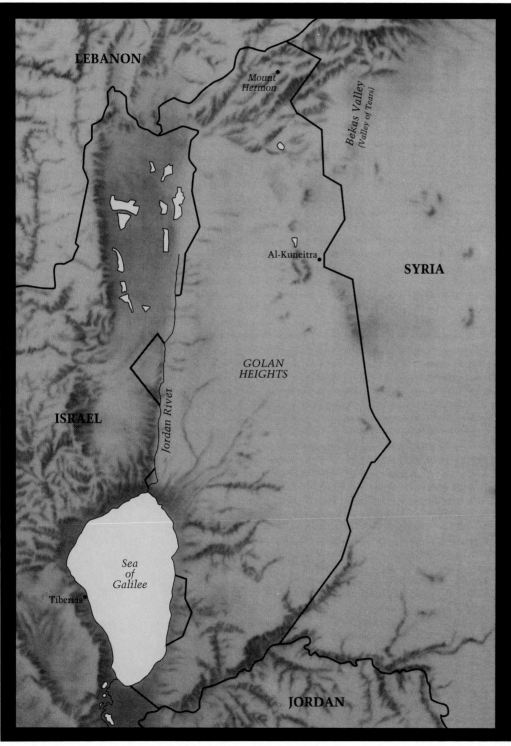

Stretching thirty-five miles from snowy Mount Hermon on the Lebanese border down to the Sea of Galilee and the Jordanian frontier, the Golan Heights forms a natural bulwark against Israel's most intractable foe, Syria. The two nations' armies were separated by a broad, shallow basin, which was the scene of the heaviest fighting on the Golan front and consequently earned the name Valley of Tears. Focal point of the Syrian offensive was the region's capital, Al-Kuneitra. As war broke out, the Israeli forces were deployed north and south of Al-Kuneitra in border fortifications along the frontier known as the Purple Line. Not more than twenty miles behind the front lay the Jordan valley and the rich agricultural lands of northern Israel.

LEBANON

Mount
Hermon

Bekas Valley
(Valley of Tears)

Al-Kuneitra

SYRIA

GOLAN
HEIGHTS

Jordan River

ISRAEL

Sea
of
Galilee

Tiberias

JORDAN

soldiers observed Syrians pulling aside camouflage netting from their tanks and artillery pieces. Within minutes, shells from 153 artillery batteries were raining down on Israeli positions. More than a hundred Syrian jet planes streaked overhead to unload their bombs on military encampments and road junctions. Israeli infantrymen ducked for cover while tank crews clambered into their vehicles and roared off to their assigned sectors in a choking swirl of dust. The barrage continued unabated for almost an hour. Then the Syrian armor appeared, flooding across the valley. One Israeli tank commander later remarked, "I never knew there were so many tanks in the world."

The assault force consisted of a wave of three mechanized infantry divisions followed by a second wave of two tank divisions. Each was a mix of tank units and infantry units mounted in armored personnel carriers; the proportion of one to the other determined the designation. In position along the Purple Line north and south of the city of Al-Kuneitra, capital of the Golan region and located in the center of the front, the Israelis had two infantry and two tank battalions of the Barak Brigade, making the initial odds at the front about ten to one.

Behind the Purple Line was the crack Seventh Brigade, the premier unit of the Israeli Armored Corps. This force, the only mobile reserve on hand, had been transferred from the Sinai and rushed to the Golan the day before, as signs of Syrian preparation for war accumulated. A week earlier the brigade commander, Colonel Avigdor Ben-Gal, with remarkable prescience, had brought all his battalion commanders to the Golan for a familiarization tour. Now his foresight was about to pay off.

As the storm broke over the Golan, his officers hurriedly set their units in motion. Lieutenant Colonel Yos Eldar commanded an integrated battalion of tanks and infantry in Ben-Gal's brigade. He sent his thinly armored APCs to the rear and moved the tanks to ramps in his assigned sector north of Al-Kuneitra.

The tank ramps used by Eldar and the other battalions were ingeniously devised to provide both shelter and interlocking fields of fire. They were three-tiered affairs, with the lowest step, just above ground level, offering the tank complete protection from direct fire but allowing the tank commander to observe the area in his front from the hatch. The second step of the ramp put the tank in a hull-down position, permitting it to fire while exposing only its turret. The highest level unmasked the tank to a greater degree but allowed it to depress its main gun sufficiently to engage the enemy at close range.

On Eldar's right flank was the tank battalion of Lieutenant Colonel Avigdor Kahalani, who learned of the outbreak of hostilities when he was strafed and bombed by Syrian MiGs on his way to a briefing. He immediately returned to his unit, spread his tanks out in a loose formation to present a less tempting target, and led them toward a ridge that dominated the terrain northeast of Al-Kuneitra. The curtain of artillery fire preceding the advance of the Syrian armored columns was a serious threat to the Israeli defenders. Kahalani ordered his tank commanders to duck inside their turrets during the worst of the shelling. Meanwhile, on his right, Eldar requested the brigade's self-propelled 155-mm guns to engage the Syrians in counterbattery fire. Then he waited for the Syrian armor to close within range of his tanks' guns.

Firing from Concealment

A tank greatly improves its chances of survival on the battlefield by presenting the smallest possible target to enemy gunners. The Soviets, leading practitioners of this theory, build tanks with squat turrets that afford little space between the tube of the main gun and the hull, or body, of the tank. The design works well when tanks are on the attack and firing across level terrain or uphill at the enemy. But on defense, when hiding behind a hill or dug into defensive positions, Western tanks with their higher turrets and greater gun clearance have the advantage. A Western tank can hunker hull down behind a rise and still depress its tube enough to engage an enemy at a lower elevation (*bottom left*). But a Soviet tank would have to expose itself on the crest of the hill to lower its gun to the same degree.

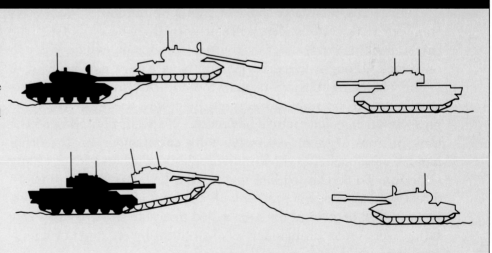

The battle about to be joined was more than just a duel between archenemies; it was a testing ground for two very different philosophies of armor—Soviet and Western. Israel's armor brigades, whose matériel came chiefly from the United States and Great Britain, had adopted the Western approach, which held that technological predominance and superior training could offset numerical deficiency. The Soviets had equipped and trained their Syrian allies in their own image, which placed emphasis on mass and firepower and stemmed from their experiences against the Wehrmacht in World War II.

The dense concentration of Syrian artillery along the Golan front exemplified the Soviet philosophy of armored warfare. By expending ammunition at a prodigious rate, the gunners effectively inhibited maneuver and deployment on the Israeli side. The Israeli artillerymen, on the other hand, relied on more sophisticated fire-control systems and a slower rate of fire from a lesser number of guns to achieve pinpoint accuracy and take out their targets.

Israeli tank training was also different. When General Israel Tal assumed command of the Armored Corps in 1964, he placed the highest priority on gunnery training, insisting that every tank gunner be an expert marksman with his 105-mm gun. He constantly pushed the limits of effective range and asserted the credo "first shot, first kill." Owing to his lofty standards, Israeli tank gunners were, as a group, probably the most accurate in the world—and Tal himself was the best of the lot.

Colonel Yos Eldar later spoke of another difference: "We always train our tank commanders to fight with their heads outside the turret, but the Syrians were trained to stay inside, where you can only look through the periscope and have a very narrow field of vision." In the rigid structure of the Syrian Army, tank commanders were given no latitude to interpret directives, to improvise, or to press an unexpected tactical advantage. They simply followed the tank in front of them. An Israeli tank commander, on the other hand, was expected to show individual initiative and adapt to any situation. To do this, he had to see what lay around him in every direction. Exposing his head outside the hatch brought grave risks, however: 90 percent of the men killed in action in Kahalani's battalion were tank commanders who were hit by shrapnel or small-arms fire while standing in their turrets.

But doctrine and tactics were not the whole story. For the first time, modern armored fighting vehicles built by the Soviets would be pitted against those of British and American design. As in tactics, a dichotomy was evident. Soviet tanks were cheap, simple, heavily armored machines. Little or no thought was given to the comfort of the crews. The M48s, M60s, and Centurions of the Israelis were, by comparison, comfortable and spacious, making it

Israeli battalion commanders Yos Eldar *(left)* and Avigdor Kahalani confer atop Kahalani's Centurion tank in the Valley of Tears. Eldar's bandages cover head and shoulder wounds that sent him to the hospital on the opening day of the Yom Kippur War. This picture was taken two days later, after he sneaked away from the medics to rejoin his unit. Both men were in the thick of the fighting throughout the war and both rose to general's rank afterward.

possible for tank crews to fight and live in their machines for more extended periods. As one Israeli sergeant explained, "In American tanks, you have the feeling they design the crew space first, then build the tank around it." Lessening crew fatigue pays important dividends in combat efficiency when the battle has dragged on for a long period of time. Moreover, the Western tanks were easier to operate. Said Kahalani, "For the driver, everything is automatic. It's like an American car: You just put it in drive. Driving the T-62 or T-55 is like driving a tractor." Also, because of the crew configuration in the turret, the loader in these Russian-built tanks sat to the right of the breech and had to load the main gun left-handed, thus slowing the rate of fire.

But the Soviet tanks had their pluses. They had good engines, they maneuvered well, and with their thick, well-sloped armor, they were difficult to penetrate. Still, neither Kahalani nor any other Israeli tanker on the Golan would have traded his Centurion for a Soviet tank, about twelve hundred of which were now headed for the Purple Line and few more than a hundred Israeli tanks. The moment of truth had arrived—the acid test of quality versus quantity. The result would be of vital interest not only to Tel Aviv and Damascus but also to Washington and Moscow.

As the Syrian columns reached the antitank ditch on the western side of the valley, they ran into a bottleneck. In contrast to the skillful synchrony of Egyptian combat engineers and assault troops in the Sinai, the wave of Syrian tanks and APCs reached their first objective with the engineers' bridging vehicles—each one a T-55 chassis with an unfolding twenty-yard section of roadway mounted on top—nowhere in sight. The infantry was forced to dismount and try to improvise crossings, breaking down the sides of the ditch with shovels. Without the protection of their APCs, the Syrian soldiers were vulnerable to small-arms fire. And, at ranges of about 2,000 yards, the stalled tanks were easy pickings for the Israeli gunners. When the bridging equipment at last appeared, the Israelis, recognizing its significance, switched their fire to these vehicles and set several ablaze. Sergeant Doron Gelber explained, "You have to decide in seconds which tank is most important to get. It was obvious we had to first destroy all the bridging tanks."

But the odds were close to ten to one, and the Israelis couldn't indefinitely stave off the Syrians, who managed to get across the ditch by sheer force of numbers. With their first line of defense breached, the Israelis brought their outnumbered tanks to bear exactly as armor should be used on the defense: not as stationary pillboxes but as a mobile strike force thrown against the enemy once his *Schwerpunkt* has been identified. This display of defensive skill came as much from instinct as from drill. Avigdor Kahalani would later point out that "in training before the Yom Kippur War, 90 percent of the time was spent on offense and only 10 percent dealt with defense." Yos Eldar, fighting beside Kahalani in the northern Golan, would concur. Israeli training, Eldar said, focused almost exclusively on the attack "in order to move the combat to the enemy's area, not to fight among the villages and kibbutzim. We improvised our defense. We were very few and we had to keep moving from area to area."

As dusk fell on October 6, Syrian pressure mounted at several points along the front—and darkness exposed what would prove to be a critical Israeli shortcoming. Syrian tanks were equipped with infrared projectors that allowed their commanders and gunners, using special sights, to engage targets in total darkness. The Israeli Armored Corps, with limited resources and a belief that such expensive equipment would not be needed (it had proved unnecessary in the Six-Day War), had decided that it could largely do without. Although the Israeli battalions each had a handful of infrared scopes for company and battalion commanders, there were no projectors and no gunsights. To fight at night,

Anticipating battle, a force of Israeli Centurion tanks assembles on the rocky Golan Heights. The large *V* on the fourth tank from the left marks it as a member of the second battalion, in this instance of a reserve brigade sent forward on October 8. A similar shape visible on two other tanks signifies first battalion. Other markings indicate a tank's company and which vehicles carry commanders so that they can be identified at a distance.

they depended on tank-mounted spotlights—a perilous practice—or on artillery star shells, illumination rounds that proved to be in critically short supply.

The fighting continued throughout the night, and the situation grew increasingly confused for the commanders on both sides as the Syrians succeeded in penetrating the Purple Line and mingled with Israeli units. Tanks engaged each other at point-blank range, flashes from their main guns illuminating the scene like strobe lights.

Some hair-raising encounters occurred that night on the rocky slopes of the Golan. A short distance behind the front in the southern sector of the heights, the commander of the Barak Brigade, Colonel Yitzhak Ben-Shoham, noticed a tank speeding to the rear without lights. Thinking that it was an Israeli crew abandoning the fight, he ordered the vehicle stopped. One of his officers managed to flag it down a mere ten yards from Ben-Shoham's vehicle. But as this officer started talking to the driver, he realized that the tank was Syrian. The crew, lost and just as unnerved by the confrontation as the Israelis, quickly buttoned up the hatches and disappeared into the blackness.

Not far away, an Israeli supply column of fuel and ammunition trucks picking its way through the gloom stopped at a crossroads to allow a lengthy tank column to pass. To the officer in charge, it seemed that Israel could not have so many tanks in one place. Stunned by the realization that these must be Syrian tanks, he and his men waited in taut silence as an entire battalion of enemy armor

slowly rattled by. Farther down the same road, one fearless officer, Lieutenant Uri Kushinari, a company commander serving with a unit of armored personnel carriers, used the darkness to his advantage. He drew his vehicles off the road and out of sight as the Syrian column approached. Then he walked up to one of the tanks, climbed aboard, pulled open a hatch, and dropped two hand grenades inside. As he raced back to his APC, the tank exploded in a ball of flame. His company withdrew through the darkness and confusion without being detected.

In general, however, the night proved to be more of an ally to the Syrians, because of their infrared equipment. In the northern sector, Kahalani and his battalion waited in the darkness as the Syrians crept forward. Through Kahalani's viewing scope, the infrared beams from the enemy tanks shone brightly, but his gunner, without an infrared-sensitive sight, could not target them. By radio, Kahalani pleaded with his artillery officer and then with his brigade commander, Colonel Ben-Gal, for illumination. They replied that no star shells were available. He tried aiming a shot himself, using the commander's override to traverse the turret and line up the target for his gunner, but the technique was ineffective. Raising the infrared viewer again to his eyes, he was horrified to see his own tank bathed in light. A Syrian was targeting him at that very moment. He yelled at his driver to back up—fast. The response seemed glacially slow in coming, but his tank succeeded in eluding the beam. Kahalani and every other Israeli tanker could only hold on and wait for the sunrise to end this terror.

In the southern Golan, the Syrians had made greater progress than they had against Kahalani's and Eldar's forces in the north. A Syrian mechanized infantry division discovered one unguarded road in the overstretched Israeli defenses south of Al-Kuneitra. Reserves that were rushing up from Israel to the Golan were still too far away to help, and the Barak Brigade, manning the tattered Purple Line defenses, had nothing left. Ben-Gal's Seventh Brigade was called upon to plug the gap. At that moment, Ben-Gal had just a single company of tanks to spare.

This company set up a classic tank ambush. Deploying in a zigzag pattern—the first tank on one side of the route, the second on the other, and so on—they waited until the tail of the Syrian column drew even with them before opening fire. They destroyed twenty-five T-55s without loss to themselves.

But even a victory of this magnitude could not stem the Syrian tide. The Barak Brigade's deputy commander was killed in his tank while charging a company of T-62s. A short while later, the brigade's operations officer and its commander, Colonel Ben-Shoham, passed a smoking, disabled Syrian tank, thinking that it had been abandoned. But one member of the Syrian crew was still inside. He fired the tank's machine gun at the two Israelis as they stood exposed in the turret of their Centurion tank, killing them instantly. The three ranking officers in the brigade were now dead, the troops exhausted and leaderless.

Syrian units reached the western edge of the Golan escarpment shortly after dawn on October 7. A full-scale breakthrough seemed imminent. But now the opposed philosophies of armored warfare would play a pivotal role. Syrian commanders were trained in the Russian doctrine to proceed against the enemy in step-by-step fashion: Once an objective was attained, the attacking units were to stop, consolidate, and bring up support before moving on. Yos Eldar would later recall an interchange he overheard on the Syrian radio net. An armored brigade that broke through in the southern sector came to a spot that offered the Syrian commander a view of the Israeli town of Tiberias on the Sea of Galilee far below. He reported this to his superior and asked permission to advance. "The Syrian division commander said, 'Stay there, don't move,'" Eldar recounted, "and this order to stay gave us the opportunity to counterattack and drive them back. They were ten minutes from the Jordan River, but their doctrine did not allow them to take advantage of our weakness and exploit opportunities."

While the advance Syrian units sat on their hands waiting for authorization to continue, Israeli reserves began to arrive in significant numbers, hitting the flank of the Syrian penetration and bringing their assault to a standstill. The battle would continue without pause for four days, but the Syrians' best chance at defeating Israel and regaining the Golan had already slipped away. On October 9, the Israelis stopped the Syrians for good, then counterattacked with a vengeance. Israeli tanks began to move forward in their more accustomed role of attack. At war's end, they would be only sixteen miles from Damascus.

By then, the valley in front of the Purple Line was a vast graveyard

A shattered hulk is all that remains of an Israeli Centurion tank after the battle on the Golan Heights; the tank was struck by a Syrian antitank round that penetrated the armor and set off ammunition or fuel stored inside. In the inset, Syrian T-55s and T-62s litter the antitank ditch that served as Israel's first line of defense. Tanks climbing out of the ditch bared their lightly armored undersides to waiting Israeli gunners.

of charred, smoldering tanks. Around the antitank ditch, the hulks were so thick that many touched one another. Every Israeli tank on the Golan had been hit at least once during the battles there; 250 had been disabled, 100 of these damaged beyond repair. But the Syrians had lost 867 tanks and the campaign as well. In the high-stake test of armored quantity versus quality, the winner was clear.

Turning the Tables in the Desert

Sunrise in the Sinai on October 14 found the Egyptians and Israelis in much the same positions they had held since the third day of the war. All along the Canal, the Egyptian bridgehead extended about ten miles into the peninsula, spread out over a bleak expanse of dunes and low plateaus.

But the disposition of forces at the front was changing. Israeli reserves—at last including sufficient infantry—were arriving in the Sinai and about 700 tanks were now on hand. Meanwhile, General Ismail, the Egyptian commander in chief, had shifted his main reserve to the east bank, bringing across the Canal 500 of the 700 tanks that had been held back in Egypt proper.

The Israeli high command, knowing that the hour of greatest danger on the Golan front had passed, was also contemplating a crossing of the Canal. Every day from the eighth to the fourteenth of October, recalled Major Giora Lev, an armored-battalion commander at the front, "we studied air recon photos and maps. I was preparing my unit for the big day." Such a counterthrust had long been incorporated into Israel's strategic war plans, and the operational aspects had been rehearsed in prewar exercises. But the military leaders were divided over the timing. Some, with characteristic Israeli élan, argued for grabbing the initiative immediately. Others counseled patience, stressing the grievous losses suffered in the opening days of the war. Because the front, separated from Israel itself by 120 miles of desert and mountains, was safely distant, these voices of caution argued that the Armored Corps should let the Egyptians make the next move.

President Assad of Syria urged the same thing; the Egyptians should turn up the pressure and draw Israeli forces from the Golan to the Sinai. His own forces were in desperate need of relief. For his part, Sadat was fully aware that time was not on his side. So far, the

Egyptian Saggers and RPGs had enjoyed great success in fending off Israeli armor, and SAMs on both sides of the Canal had provided an effective shield against Israeli aircraft. But with the tide turning on the Golan, Israel would be able soon to transfer some of its power to the Sinai and perhaps end the standoff there. Opting to go on the offensive, the Egyptians moved their Fourth and 21st Armored Divisions across the Canal in a bid to gain control of access routes, including the strategically important Gidi and Mitla passes, leading to Israeli command and supply headquarters in the central Sinai.

At six o'clock on the morning of the fourteenth, a ninety-minute artillery barrage heralded the showdown. Then the Sinai reverberated with the distinctive crack of high-velocity tank guns and the gut-churning, hollow thunk of projectiles striking metal as more than fifteen hundred Egyptian and Israeli tanks slugged it out in a melee of armor unmatched since Soviet and German forces met in the pivotal Battle of Kursk on Russian soil in 1943.

The commander of the First Egyptian Armored Brigade, 21st Armored Division, was confident of victory as he surveyed his formation from the cupola of his lurching armored personnel carrier. Artillery fire was preceding his advance as scheduled, blanketing the enemy's defenses with a deadly rain of high explosive and flying metal. But as he neared the Israeli positions, suddenly all hell broke loose. Squinting into the rising sun through the smoke and dust of the artillery bombardment, the commander could not pinpoint the source of the fire that now enveloped his brigade from many directions at once. His tanks and APCs were hit one after another and started to burn. Some of the tanks exploded, blowing the heavy turrets high into the air to land beside the shattered hulls. Some of the APCs, trying desperately to escape, overturned and spilled infantry onto the sand, where they were cut down by machine-gun fire. In mere minutes, the brigade was decimated, its shocked and demoralized remnants making for the rear at top speed. More waves, more brigades followed, only to smash themselves against the Israelis who, unseen, could not be fired upon.

On the Israeli side, Lieutenant Yuval Neria, who had been in action since the opening day of the war, watched the Egyptian advance in awe. There were so many tanks and APCs approaching his position behind the crest of a line of dunes that he ordered his men to open fire at the extreme range of more than two and a half miles. And still the Egyptians "came toward us without stopping and shooting, just moving. It was suicide coming from the low ground along the Canal up to us."

The Israeli tankers were able to engage the advancing Egyptians from behind the dunes in part because of their equipment. Their British- and American-made tanks had a higher profile than the Soviet-built T-55s and T-62s. Although the extra height presented a larger target when fully exposed, it also enabled the Israelis to point their guns downward as much as ten degrees (versus four degrees for Soviet tanks). This was a crucial advantage in undulating terrain: A tank could hide behind a dune in a position that angled its hull upward, yet fire on the enemy by depressing the gun.

North of Neria's position, Major Giora Lev saw the Egyptians rolling toward his battalion in waves, "company after company, without any idea of how to conduct an armored battle." He opened fire at two miles and knocked out one tank after another. Still the Egyptians pushed on until, by sheer weight of numbers, they were finally in among Lev's tanks. "They broke the line without firing. They just drove. We shot them at a range of fifty meters." His battalion savaged the tanks that penetrated the line, destroying more than 60 in an hour. "There were burning tanks everywhere. We saw the crews jumping out and running away."

The Egyptian tanks were accompanied by infantry in droves. Lev called in mortars and artillery to drive them back. This time, the advancing Egyptians were out in the open rather than in the foxholes that had made them so difficult to kill in their defensive perimeter. "I didn't want the infantry to get as close to us as the tanks because they had RPGs, which are very dangerous." Lev used his own infantry ("they were my eyes because we were busy") to guard his flanks and provide protection against Saggers.

Lieutenant Doron Hoek commanded a company of tanks guarding the Gidi Pass. In his sector, the attack started with a single-armored scout

Hastening to the battle raging along the Suez Canal, a column of Israeli M60s takes to the sand in order to avoid a traffic jam on the Akavish road. These tanks, all of which belong to the same company, as indicated by the inverted Vs on the turrets, were destroyed a few hours later in fierce fighting at the Chinese Farm.

car racing at full speed toward the waiting Israelis. When the vehicle was within 350 yards, one of Hoek's tanks fired. "All the gunner had to do was pull the trigger to hit it." The reckless armored car was followed by tanks slowly crawling toward Hoek; with them came thousands of infantry on foot. "It was either heroic or foolish, I'm not sure which," he said later.

As with the other Israeli units that day, Hoek's tanks occupied good fire positions on high ground. His gunners lit up the Egyptian tanks in quick succession, but the rest continued to drive forward relentlessly until they, too, were mingled with the Israeli tanks. "It was frightening because they did not stop," Hoek recalled. Of his company, only his own tank was hit. An armor-piercing shell slammed into the turret ring and jammed the traverse mechanism. He pulled out of the line to change tanks, and by the time he got back, the Egyptians were retreating.

Hoek terms the action a "massacre" and cites as the primary cause the Egyptians' failure to take the Israeli tanks under fire from a distance before advancing. In fact, Israeli eyewitnesses all along the front remark that the Egyptians never stopped to fire during the attack. Of course, the Israelis, hull down behind the dunes, were not easy prey, but the Egyptians, "by rolling forward, revealed the whole height of their tanks and made themselves easy targets," Hoek explains. "When they get to a distance of fifteen hundred meters every shell you fire should hit, and most of them did."

With the Egyptian spearhead finally blunted, Neria's brigade commander ordered him to descend from the hill and pursue the retreating enemy. He immediately ran into Egyptians jumping from the tanks and APCs. "And then I found myself involved in very dirty work, killing them from very close range. Some of our tanks ran over them with their treads."

October 14 marked the Egyptians' first attempt at a large-scale armored offensive, and their inexperience was clearly evident. The valor of the individual tank crews was indisputable, but the collective might of two armored divisions had been frittered away in piecemeal attacks that gained nothing. The Egyptians made several tactical mistakes that day, the combined effects of which served to doom their attack from the start. The armored brigades launched disconnected, uncoordinated assaults at nine points along the front, which enabled the Israelis to deal with each attack separately. There was no identifiable *Schwerpunkt*.

A concentrated effort against one of the passes, grouping all the brigades along a narrow axis of attack, might possibly have punched through the Israeli defenses. But by trying to gain all their objectives at once, the Egyptians were condemned to failure. Another point frequently mentioned by Israeli tankers is that the Egyptians—using standard Russian armored doctrine—attacked in echelons, one wave following another, thus giving the defenders breathing space and time to replenish ammunition between attacks.

By day's end, well over 400 wrecked, smoldering Egyptian armored vehicles littered the Sinai. About forty Israeli tanks had been hit, but only six of them were damaged beyond repair. The Israeli high command, certain now that the enemy's offensive strength was broken, eagerly moved to put its plan for the final phase of the war into motion.

Counterthrust into the Land of the Pharaohs

The Egyptian offensive on October 14 played right into the Israelis' hands. Egypt had committed its armored reserve to the Sinai, and the Israeli tankers had shattered it. Now the Armored Corps could operate in its preferred style, using maneuver, deep penetration, and surprise to ensure that the end game of the Sinai campaign would be played out in a different venue altogether—on the west bank of the Suez Canal.

After occupying the Sinai in 1967, Israeli engineers had laid out an assembly area for pontoon-bridge sections just behind the sand rampart running along the east bank of the Canal. A stretch of the rampart itself was thinned, and the weakened section was marked so that it could be readily found and bulldozed to let bridging equipment and tanks through. The engineers also constructed two roads, known as Akavish and Tirtur, to carry the bridge sections from Tasa, an Israeli forward supply depot that lay about twenty miles northeast of the assembly area.

The focal point of these preparations was the northern end of the Great Bitter Lake. Plans called for Israeli forces to penetrate Egypt at this central location, should the need ever arise, to allow room for movement up or down the west bank of the Canal. The lake itself would protect the left flank of the bridgehead against counterattack. But to carry out the crossing, the Armored Corps would first have to open a corridor through the Egyptian lines and clear the Akavish and Tirtur roads so that the needed equipment could be brought to the scene.

Fittingly, the crossing was entrusted to Ariel Sharon. This controversial general, who in previous wars had earned a reputation for daring (some say recklessness), had worked out the details of the crossing when he was running the Sinai command. At his disposal were three armored brigades, a brigade of infantry, including some paratroopers, and a force of engineers with earthmoving machinery, rafts for ferrying tanks, and the floating bridge. Straddling Tirtur and Akavish, blocking the way to the Canal, were an Egyptian armored division—now consisting of about 200 tanks—and an infantry division equipped with antitank missiles. "The problem," Sharon said later, "was how to reach the water and establish the bridgehead in the same night. We had to do it before daylight, because if we lost surprise, no doubt we would have found quite a number of tanks waiting for us on the other side."

At 5:00 p.m. on October 15, Sharon began to move. A diversionary thrust due west from Tasa toward the Canal-side city of Ismailia drew the attention of the Egyptian Second Army away from the vicinity of the main attack. One of Sharon's armored brigades then set off after dark through the trackless dunes south of the Akavish road on a nineteen-mile break for the Canal. Reconnaissance had determined that the area coincided with the seam between the Egyptian Second Army, which held the front from this point north to the Mediterranean coast, and the Third Army, whose sector stretched south to the Gulf of Suez. Unit boundaries are always the weakest link in a front because two different command, communication, and supply networks stretch back from one spot to different headquarters.

The Israeli armor was able to slip through the gap undetected. When it reached the shore of the Great Bitter Lake, the brigade split into its three component battalions and turned north. One battalion went to check on the crossing site. A second returned toward Tasa along the Tirtur and Akavish roads to take the Egyptians from the rear and open the route for the bridging equipment. The third battalion continued up the east bank of the Canal to act as a flank guard for the Israeli units that would soon be moving down the Akavish-Tirtur corridor.

This last battalion, including the ubiquitous Lieutenant Yuval Neria, ran into trouble almost immediately. Less than a mile beyond the crossing site, the unit stumbled into the reserve formations of the entire Second Army. The stillness of the night was shattered as a firefight erupted at point-blank range around an experimental agricultural station known as the Chinese Farm. (Before the Six-Day War, irrigation experiments had been carried out there by Japanese experts; when Israeli troops overran the farm, they found equipment bearing inscriptions that they mistakenly took for Chinese.) Soon all three battalions of the brigade were drawn into a vortex of battle centered on the area. Tanks and armored personnel carriers roared around in the dark, trying to distinguish friend from foe. Dozens of vehicles were hit and set ablaze. "Although it was night, after fifteen minutes you could see everything like daylight," remembered Neria. Suddenly "my tank was lifted up into the air by a very massive explosion," said Neria. "I wasn't hurt, but my driver was wounded." The tank had struck a mine.

He evacuated his crew on another tank, then set off on foot to catch up with the rest of his company, working his way through the groves and fields of the Chinese Farm. He heard Egyptians all around him. After a seeming eternity, he reached his comrades, only to discover that they were cut off from the rest of their brigade. Neria would remain with them in that spot for the next two and a half days while his brigade's tank force was whittled down from a hundred to no more than two dozen. "We stayed there defending against Egyptians coming from north to south, trying to get to the bridgehead. Their attacks were like waves every few hours."

Sergeant Haim Rabinovitch, a tank commander in another unit that fought at the Chinese Farm, later recalled feeling "like cannon fodder. We were to keep the Egyptians busy in order to let other forces get through on the Tirtur axis." His battalion, too, took very

An Israeli F-4 Phantom, returning from a bombing run along the Suez Canal, flashes over a Centurion towing a raft toward the Canal. The motorized rafts, each capable of carrying one tank, were indispensable in floating armor across the Canal before pontoon bridges could be brought up and assembled.

heavy losses. "I remember the Egyptian infantry sitting in hundreds of foxholes shooting missiles." Like other tankers in this war, Rabinovitch found that fighting infantry at close range was no uplifting experience. "If they were close, we would throw hand grenades, and a few times we ran over them." He had four tanks shot out from under him, losing three to Saggers and one to a direct hit from a 122-mm mortar. "I managed to survive, I don't know how. From my original crew, the driver lost his leg and the rest were killed."

Despite Rabinovitch's experience, the Israeli tankers by this point in the war had learned effective methods of dealing with Saggers, and losses to this new weapon never again approached the level of the first three days of combat. Lieutenant Neria explained, "The sight of the Sagger was common to me by this point. I knew them from the first day."

The missile was easy for tank commanders to spot from their cupolas. According to Neria, "It has a balloon of flame like fireworks out the back, and it spins as it travels three or four meters from the ground. It makes a lot of noise and appears to be moving in slow motion. The Sagger is very frightening, but its slow movement gives me the feeling I can survive, I can avoid it, if I move only two or three meters with my tank at the appropriate time. The problem is, you have to move when it is two thirds of the distance to you. Then you don't give the man who sent it the opportunity to remaneuver the missile."

Another technique was for the tank commander to fire his machine gun in the direction from which the missile was approaching. It was not necessary to hit the operator, merely to make him duck for cover and take his eye off the optical sight with which he guided the missile. But although tankers now had a method of dealing with this latest wrinkle in armored warfare, they still had plenty of threats to worry about: artillery, other tanks' main guns, and the infantry's close-range RPGs. All were in abundance.

The combat around the Chinese Farm was as ferocious as any in the war. After a visit to the scene in the wake of the fighting, Defense Minister Moshe Dayan wrote, "I could not hide my emotions. Hundreds of mutilated and burned-out war vehicles lay strewn over the fields, some still giving off smoke. There were Israeli tanks and Egyptian tanks, only a few yards away from each other, and abandoned supply transports, caught in the act of flight.

"I am no novice at war or battle scenes," Dayan continued, "but

I have never seen such a sight. Here was a vast field of slaughter stretching all around as far as the eye could see. The tanks, the armored personnel carriers, the guns, and the ammunition trucks crippled, overturned, burned, and smoking were grim evidence of the frightful battle that had been fought here."

The coincidental positioning of the bulk of the Second Army's reserves around the Chinese Farm that night had caused the Israelis many anxious moments, but Egyptian attempts to squeeze off the corridor over the next few days were hampered by the divided Egyptian command structure. Had the attacks of the Second and Third armies on either side of the breach been better coordinated, the spearhead of the Israeli column strung out along the Akavish road might have been cut off and the crossing attempt thwarted.

In one of these Egyptian attacks against the northern flank of the corridor, Yuval Neria's tank was hit again, and this time his luck finally ran out. "I think it was a 180-mm gun; it was a big, big shell." One of his crew was killed immediately, and the rest, including Neria, were severely injured. He was evacuated, suffering from wounds to his foot and back and burns on his face and hands. In two weeks of unremitting combat, Neria had changed tanks eleven times. For his actions throughout the war—from the opening day along the Bar-Lev Line to the hell of the Chinese Farm—he would receive Israel's highest decoration, the Medal of Valor.

Even as Neria and Rabinovitch were fighting their desperate battle around the Chinese Farm, Major Giora Lev, who had been preparing his battalion for the crossing since October 8, was running the gauntlet down the Akavish road, towing motorized rafts from Tasa. "The Egyptians shot at us from both sides, trying to close the corridor, but we managed to pass through." He reached the Canal about midnight on the fifteenth, the first armored unit on the scene. There, he was ordered to support a paratroop brigade that had crossed earlier that night in assault boats. Because the bridging sections were stuck in a massive traffic jam far up the Akavish, Lev would have to get across on the rafts, each of which was capable of carrying one tank. None of his tank commanders had experience with this conveyance, so he decided to wait until first light to cross.

At dawn, combat engineers breached the sand rampart with a bulldozer tank, pushed the motorized rafts into the water and made them fast to the shore. Lev's battalion then began the delicate task of driving a fifty-four-ton tank onto a float barely wide enough for the tracks. "You have to load onto the raft backward so you can get off going forward." Despite the fierce battle raging behind him at the Chinese Farm, the crossing site itself was as quiet as peacetime. In the tank behind Lev, the commander jokingly bent his radio antenna down toward the water as though he were fishing.

Lev's was the first Israeli tank across the Canal. Two hundred yards beyond the west bank he encountered an Egyptian APC, the first sign of the enemy. He considers himself fortunate that he didn't meet resistance at the water's edge when his tanks were helpless aboard the rafts. "If we had crossed twenty minutes later it could have been too late. Sometimes you have to have luck." But luck favors the bold, and an armored commander needs to be bold to the point of audacity. Moving a substantial force to the west bank while the corridor was still under heavy attack, as Sharon did, was a risky venture to say the least. A cautious, rigidly structured army trained in the Russian principle of consolidating forces and moving step by step certainly never would have tried it. But the Israeli Armored Corps was none of those things, and the gamble paid off. By nine o'clock that morning, thirty tanks and two thousand men had been ferried over.

Substantially reinforcing this body depended on the bridging equipment, which would not reach the crossing site until the following day, so vigorous was the enemy's resistance along the Tirtur-Akavish corridor. Sharon's superiors ordered him to dig in and protect the bridgehead until additional armor and infantry could be brought across. But the maverick general had other ideas. He decided to strike off behind Egyptian lines to create the maximum possible disruption. Ignoring protests from headquarters, he broke his meager force into raiding parties, leaving a small security force to guard the bridgehead.

Even though operating in full daylight, Sharon's men still had the advantage of surprise. Egyptian intelligence initially believed that the intruders were a reconnaissance unit of no great consequence. Evidently they saw the events of the night—the Israeli feint toward Ismailia, the thrust along the roads from Tasa to the Great Bitter Lake, and the raging battle at the Chinese Farm—as isolated actions rather than components of a single plan. But the Egyptians would soon learn that they had made a mistake in taking so lightly the seemingly insignificant Israeli foothold on their territory.

Giora Lev's first target was an airfield at the town of Deversoir,

At dawn on October 18, an Israeli combat engineer stands at the bow of a tank-laden raft, directing it into the Suez Canal. Already approaching the far shore is battalion commander Giora Lev in the first Israeli tank to reach the west bank. The trees beyond the sand rampart grow in the so-called green belt, a lush area bordering a freshwater channel just west of the briny Suez.

less than two miles west of the crossing site. He approached the main gate with four of his tanks. "The Egyptian MP at the gate saluted me," Lev recalled. "He had no idea what was happening. He just saw four tanks coming to the gate and he opened it." Taking the surprised sentry in tow, Lev's men ranged up and down the runway, shooting up dozens of planes, vehicles, and antiaircraft guns before the stunned Egyptians could react. "I had two mech infantry companies with me. They did a beautiful job using hand grenades and small-caliber weapons." Whimsically, Lev phoned his wife from the airfield. "She said, 'Where are you?' and I said, 'There! This is the big day! I'm sure you'll hear about it on the radio and you'll know it was me.' "

Later that morning he spoke on the radio to the deputy chief of staff, General Bar-Lev. "It was a very important moment," Lev remembers. "He ordered me to go after the missile sites. He said if I destroy the missile sites we can push our air force through the corridor." Lev's battalion raided SAM batteries ("it was like fireworks to hit the missiles") and destroyed more than a hundred armored vehicles on October 16, "and I didn't even have a single injury in my unit."

Captain David Halevy, who had gone to war on October 8 without binoculars or a map, crossed the Canal on October 17 by raft. "On the west bank, we were finally in our real capacity. We were operating in the rear of the Egyptian lines." The day after he crossed, Halevy was ordered to raid SAM batteries as Lev had done. "I built special task forces, made of two or three APCs, two or three tanks, and each of these task forces went to a SAM battery and destroyed it, smashed it.

"The tactic was to approach the SAM battery with the tanks and APCs to a distance of about two to three thousand meters. The tanks would fire a number of shells and hold positions while the APCs on the left and the right would roll very quickly into the SAM battery and open fire with their machine guns. And that worked, it worked beautifully." Halevy's unit knocked out some twelve batteries without suffering a single casualty. "Now I had a map. It was fun working with this; at least I knew where I was and what my targets were."

Such raids destroyed about 75 percent of the SAM sites on the western side of the Canal. The batteries were without any sort of armor-piercing weapons so, in desperation, the crews fired the SAMs at the Israelis as an antitank weapon. "And that's not a funny sight, you know," Halevy exclaimed. "It's like a telephone pole flying at you at very high speed." The missiles might have been frightening, but as antitank projectiles, they were completely ineffective. In no time at all the Israeli combined-arms teams such as Lev's and Halevy's opened a passage for the Israeli Air Force.

The Egyptians, now frantic, redoubled their efforts to close off the route from Tasa to the crossing point and obliterate the Israeli bridgehead. But an Israeli armored column, accompanying the bridge sections, fought its way through, and during the day of October 17, the pontoons were ready to be anchored in place.

With strong forces now advancing into both Egypt and Syria, the Israelis knew that a UN-sponsored cease-fire would soon be imposed. They wanted to improve their bargaining position before the guns fell silent. With typical daring they decided to move south from their bridgehead in divisional strength to encircle the entire Egyptian Third Army in the Sinai. The Israeli Air Force, no longer threatened by the SAMs, provided close air support.

On October 20, Halevy was operating on the Geneifa Hills above the Great Bitter Lake. Spread out below him west of the Canal was the entire rear echelon of the Third Army. "We were there behind them and they couldn't understand who was

The SA-2, a mainstay of Egyptian antiaircraft defenses, shielded President Sadat's forces in the Sinai against Israeli air attack. Lethal against aircraft, the missile was little more than a costly firework when launched at raiding Israeli armor.

Captain David Halevy stands in the turret of a T-55 taken from the Egyptians during the Sinai campaign. Halevy's reconnaissance battalion was one of several Israeli units that captured large quantities of undamaged armor from Egypt's Third Army. After the war, Halevy commanded an Israeli regiment that was composed entirely of captured T-55s.

hitting them. On that day, I got formations of Phantoms to lead the bombing. That was terrific. For the first time, I had the Air Force. I told them where I wanted bombs. I saw huge convoys of tanks and immediately I got four Phantoms. Half an hour later, I discovered a new column of trucks, I got four Skyhawks." Halevy likens the devastating impact of his combined ground-air assault to "cutting with a very sharp knife through butter. We destroyed the entire rear headquarters of the Third Army." He and his men started picking up Egyptian officers—including a paymaster with the Third Army's payroll—who seemed stunned and disoriented to find enemy armor in their midst. They also captured a substantial number of undamaged armored personnel carriers and tanks, parking some for retrieval later and giving some away. "On the twenty-second, a paratroop battalion came to me asking for Russian APCs so we gave them a quick course in driving them."

By the time the cease-fire finally took effect on October 24, Halevy's unit and others had reached Suez City at the southern terminus of the Canal. The Third Army was indeed trapped on the far side and, as negotiations progressed, depended on Israeli shipments of food and medicine to endure.

David Halevy had covered a lot of ground in the past two weeks. Remarkably, he was commanding the same armored personnel carrier—a brand-new American-built M113—in which he had set out from his mobilization depot in Israel. "I started, I think, with forty-two miles on the odometer and I finished the war with twelve hundred and sixty miles on the thing. It went through hell and it brought me back. It's the most reliable machine that was ever made, an excellent fighting vehicle."

Lieutenant Doron Hoek, who had helped stop the Egyptian tanks at the Gidi Pass on October 14, became one of the war's last casualties. On the afternoon of the twenty-second—the day the cease-fire was first declared—Hoek was in position along the main Suez-Cairo highway. Everything was peaceful, and he thought the war was over. "I very foolishly stood up in my tank in our fire position. Some Egyptian soldier approached our lines and shot an antitank missile." Hoek saw the Sagger coming, spinning slowly as it skimmed over the ground, a sight that was by now familiar to every Israeli tanker. He shouted to the driver to back up and dropped down into the turret. "It hit right where I had been standing in the commander's position. I was wounded in the head and that was the end of the war for me."

With the cessation of hostilities, the combatants paused to take stock. A great deal of damage had been wrought in a remarkably short period of time. The frenetic pace of modern armored warfare consumed men, machines, and matériel in staggering quantities. From the surprise Egyptian and Syrian attacks to the denouement on the west bank of the Canal, a mere eighteen days had passed. But those days had witnessed some battles that, for sheer intensity if not numbers involved, matched the fiercest fighting of World War II. The Egyptians and Syrians had lost around 2,000 tanks and suffered 16,000 killed in action. About 400 Israeli tanks were damaged beyond repair and more than 2,500 soldiers had died.

Some cherished notions about the tank had perished, too. Yuval Neria, who probably saw as much combat as anyone in the war,

Following a United Nations-sponsored cease-fire, Egyptian troops ferry provisions across the Suez Canal on Soviet-made BTR-50 amphibious armored personnel carriers. A ramp through the sand rampart on the opposite side of the Canal led to the beneficiaries of the supply effort—the soldiers of Egypt's vanquished Third Army.

states, "You should never use tanks by themselves. They are very vulnerable, very big targets. You cannot use them in close-range fighting against infantry." Neither he nor any other tanker is prepared to discard the tank as an anachronism. Tanks proved their worth in this war as tank killers in their own right on the Golan Heights and on October 14 in the Sinai. And when they were turned loose in the Egyptian rear across the Canal, they spread panic and sealed the fate of the Third Army. But, remembering his experiences in the opening days of the war when tanks had been sent in alone to smash through the Egyptian prepared defenses, Neria concludes that the enemy's front must be breached before sending armor through. "Tanks should be used to finish the job, not to start it."

David Halevy also had some things to say based on his experiences. "Lesson number one of the Yom Kippur War is the vitality of the combined unit made of tanks, APCs, artillery, and even reconnaissance elements." This was not a new lesson, but it had to be relearned. The combined-arms doctrine was pioneered by the first practitioners of blitzkrieg in Poland, France, and Russia. In fact, the Israeli drive down the west bank to trap the Egyptian Third Army bears a striking resemblance to the early battles of encirclement the Wehrmacht fought on the Eastern Front.

"A war is won by destroying the main bulk of the enemy's fighting elements or surrounding them," Halevy concluded, "and by concentrating your forces at the *Schwerpunkt* to reach the key strategic positions in the enemy rear. That's the whole idea behind the tank. Just ask Guderian." ★

The Violent Clash of Tank and Tank Killer

Since World War II, the main battle tank has changed considerably: Its armor is made of high-tech composites instead of plain steel, vastly improving the tank's survivability, and the caliber of its main gun has grown from 70 millimeters to 120 or 125 millimeters, providing it with greatly increased firepower. The armored giants of today are also far more mobile than their predecessors; some are propelled by engines that generate as much as 1,500 horsepower. And yet the tank remains vulnerable today, as it was fifty years ago.

The reason is simple: As the main battle tank has evolved, so too have the many devices designed to kill it. As shown on the pages that follow, some of these weapons use raw force in an effort to disable the tank's main gun, break its suspension, knock off a track, jam the turret, or pierce the vehicle's brittle shell to hurt its most vulnerable component, the crew. Other weapons, like the hand-launched Panzerfaust 3 shown exploding against the turret of the M48 below, employ massive amounts of chemical energy to accomplish the same ends. Properly used, panzerfausts can turn a lone infantryman into a giant killer.

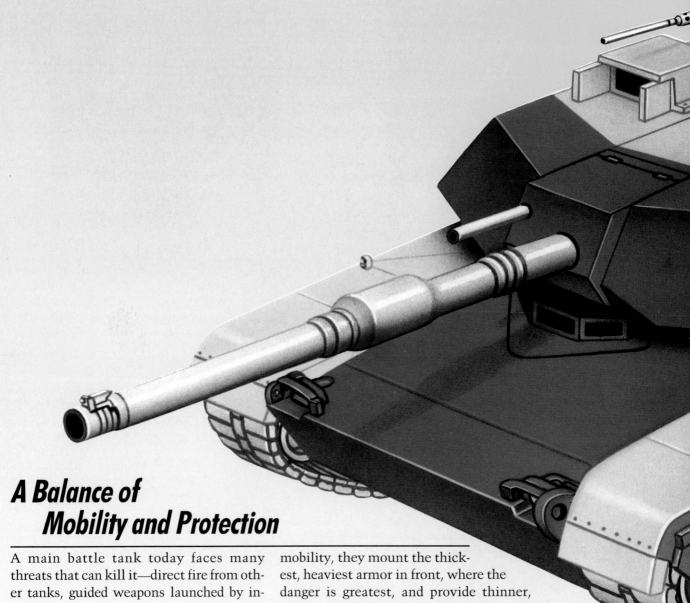

A Balance of Mobility and Protection

A main battle tank today faces many threats that can kill it—direct fire from other tanks, guided weapons launched by infantry and from helicopters, cannons shot by aircraft, artillery fire, mines. To survive, it needs armor, and lots of it. But armor, whether conventional rolled or cast nickel-chrome-molybdenum steel or the modern composite called Chobham, based on a British concept, is extremely heavy. A tank clad top to bottom with armor thick enough to counter every threat would be too weighty to move. No road or bridge could support it, and it would be nearly impossible to transport, especially by air.

Consequently, tank designers are forced to compromise. Swapping invincibility for mobility, they mount the thickest, heaviest armor in front, where the danger is greatest, and provide thinner, lighter shields elsewhere. The armor on the M1 Abrams, depicted here, was distributed with this trade-off in mind: Sloped slabs of Chobham-type laminated armor *(dark blue)* cover the nose, glacis plate, and turret front; comparatively thin layers of the same armor *(medium blue)* guard the sides of the turret and hull, and plain rolled steel *(light blue)* protects the rear and belly and the top of the turret and hull. The lighter armor leaves the M1 somewhat vulnerable to mines and top-attack weapons but preserves its mobility, which is an effective defense in itself.

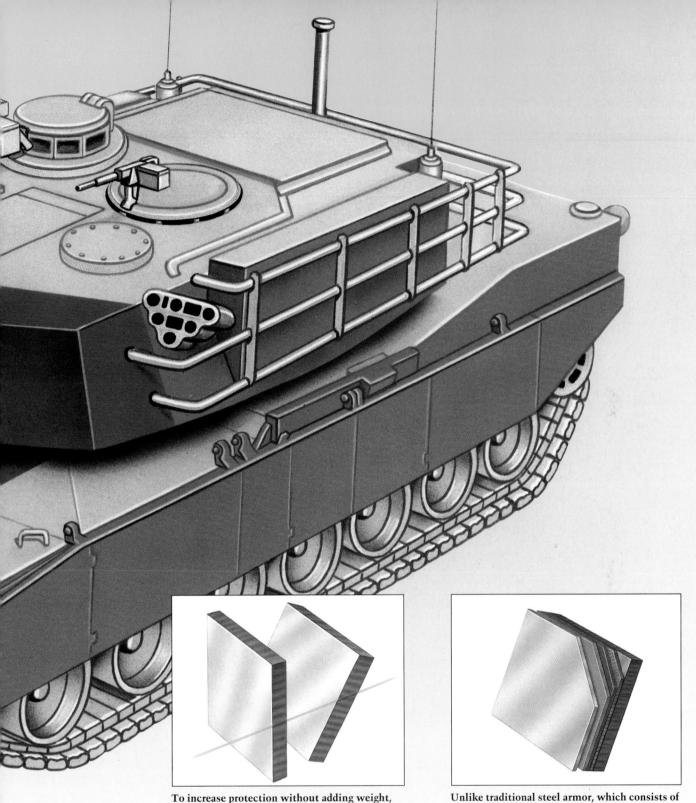

To increase protection without adding weight, designers often shield their tanks with sloped armor, which can cause a projectile with a flat trajectory to skip rather than penetrate when it strikes. Moreover, as shown above, sloping increases the distance a shot must travel to puncture the armor: Inclining 4-inch armor to a sixty-degree angle, for example, increases its horizontal thickness to 7.9 inches.

Unlike traditional steel armor, which consists of a solid mass, Chobham-type special armor, pictured above, comprises spaced layers of assorted materials. The actual composition is secret, but it may include an alloy of depleted uranium (one of the densest natural metals), heat-resistant ceramics, and hard fibers arrayed in geometric patterns inside metal or plastic. Almost three times more effective than steel alone, the layers break up projectiles and absorb and deflect the force of an explosion. The components of laminated armor can be juggled to counter different threats.

Smashing through Armor with Kinetic Energy

To disable a tank, an antitank round does more than merely pierce the armor that protects the vehicle; it wreaks havoc inside as well. One simple way to accomplish this is to hurl a metal shot against the armor: If the projectile is dense enough and its speed is high enough, it will possess sufficient kinetic energy to penetrate, bringing with it fiery fragments of armor that bounce around the interior, destroying equipment, igniting stored fuel and ammunition, and endangering the crew.

Two kinds of kinetic-energy munitions work this way. The first, known as a plate charge, is commonly employed in mines to attack a tank's lightly armored underbelly, one of its most vulnerable areas. When the charge explodes, it ejects a high-speed, cone-shaped slug that is capable of ripping through steel plate almost three inches thick—heavier than the armor that protects the bottom of even the well-armored Abrams.

The second variety comprises several types of dartlike projectiles known as rod penetrators and designed to attack a tank's heavy upper armor. Made of tungsten, tungsten carbide, or an alloy of depleted uranium, the missiles are up to twenty times longer than they are wide. The thirteen-pound shot fired from the 120-mm main gun of an M1 (below) flies at 5,000 feet per second, giving it the kinetic energy of a ten-ton truck traveling at seventy miles an hour—energy it concentrates into an impact area less than one inch in diameter.

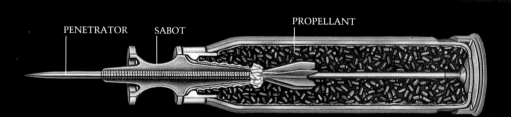

PENETRATOR   SABOT   PROPELLANT

The penetrator of the armor-piercing, fin-stabilized, discarding sabot (APFSDS) round above is much narrower than the bore of the 120-mm cannon that fires it. An aluminum alloy seal called a sabot fills the space, allowing expanding gases from burning propellant to accelerate both shot and sabot along the unrifled barrel. Muzzle blast and wind resistance peel away the pieces of the sabot after firing (left), while six aluminum fins stabilize the projectile's flight toward the target.

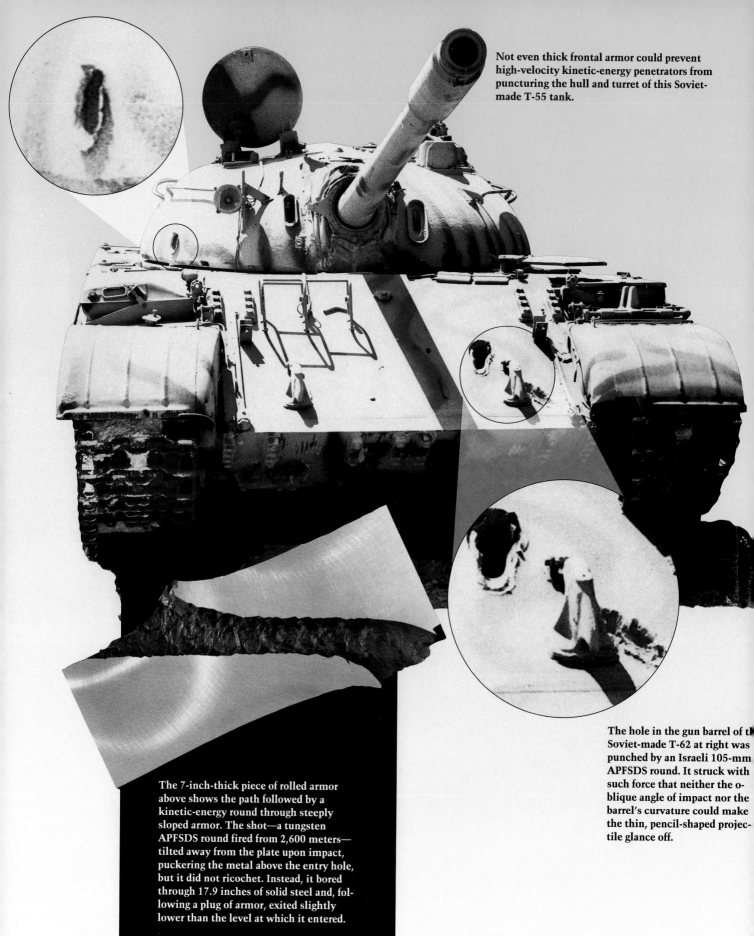

Not even thick frontal armor could prevent high-velocity kinetic-energy penetrators from puncturing the hull and turret of this Soviet-made T-55 tank.

The 7-inch-thick piece of rolled armor above shows the path followed by a kinetic-energy round through steeply sloped armor. The shot—a tungsten APFSDS round fired from 2,600 meters—tilted away from the plate upon impact, puckering the metal above the entry hole, but it did not ricochet. Instead, it bored through 17.9 inches of solid steel and, following a plug of armor, exited slightly lower than the level at which it entered.

The hole in the gun barrel of th[e] Soviet-made T-62 at right was punched by an Israeli 105-mm APFSDS round. It struck with such force that neither the o-blique angle of impact nor the barrel's curvature could make the thin, pencil-shaped projec-tile glance off.

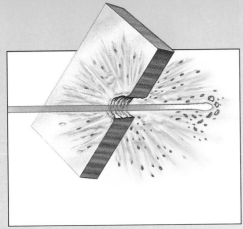

A depleted-uranium round striking conventional steel armor curls back the metal upon impact and releases brilliant white light and heat. Although the shot breaks up as it penetrates, it forces the armor to bulge inward and fail, allowing the projectile and superhot fragments of ruptured armor to enter the tank, where they ricochet wildly.

A kinetic-energy shot hitting laminated armor pierces the steel box that encloses the armor but is stopped inside. Spaced layers of depleted uranium and other materials knock the projectile off course and cause it to shear and break up. Subsequent layers absorb and deflect the pieces —which have less mass than the solid shot and thus less energy—before they enter the tank.

A Searing Jet of Gas and Molten Metal

Unlike kinetic-energy projectiles, which gain their armor-piercing momentum from the cannon that fires them, a high-explosive antitank (HEAT) round carries within it an explosive charge specially designed to knock out a tank.

As a result, a HEAT round does not need to fly at high speed in order to penetrate a tank's protective armor, and, though tanks fire such munitions, no heavy gun is required. Instead, the weapon can be delivered with precision by infantrymen equipped with portable, relatively inexpensive rocket launchers and recoilless rifles, and from helicopters, light fixed-wing aircraft, tanks, and armored personnel carriers—vehicles that use mobility and the element of surprise to compound their lethal striking power.

A HEAT round contains a warhead called a shaped charge. On detonating, it unleashes a high-speed jet of molten metal and hot gases capable of blasting through conventional steel armor many times thicker than might be expected from the size of the shell. The Soviet-made rocket-propelled grenade shown at far right, for instance, is lightweight enough to be fired from a tube resting on the gunner's shoulder. But it carries a warhead that can bore a two-inch-wide hole through steel thirteen inches thick. And once inside the tank, its jet will be strong enough to ignite stored fuel and ammunition and to scald and blind the crew.

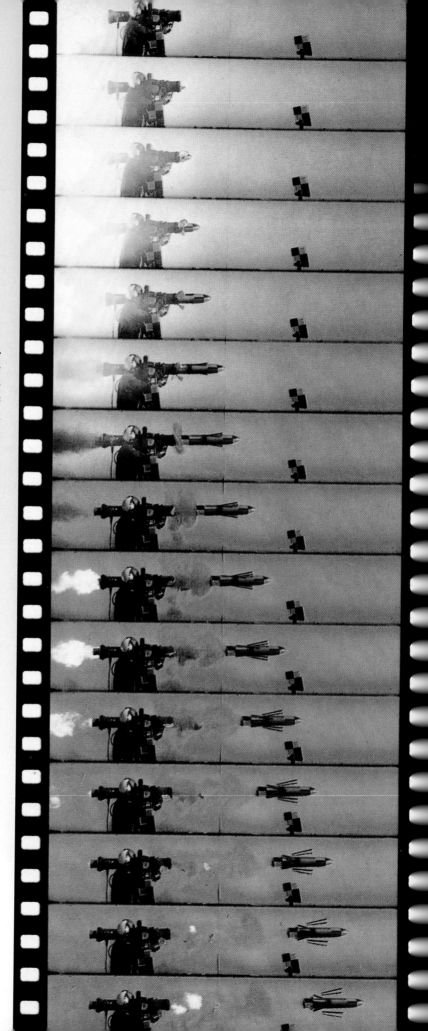

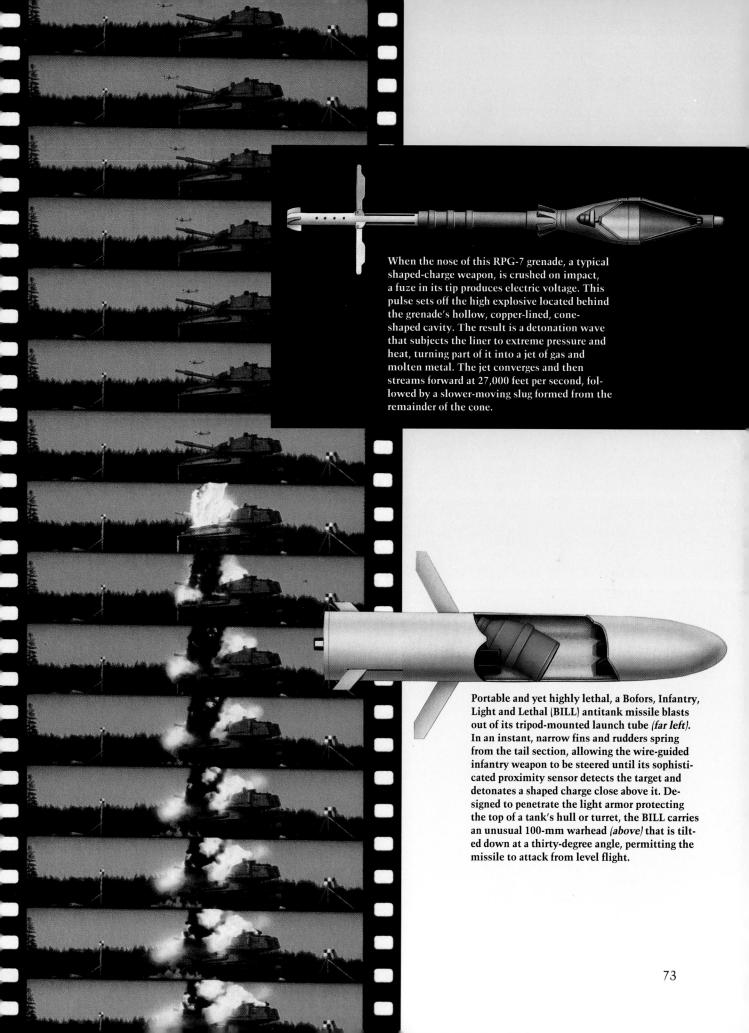

When the nose of this RPG-7 grenade, a typical shaped-charge weapon, is crushed on impact, a fuze in its tip produces electric voltage. This pulse sets off the high explosive located behind the grenade's hollow, copper-lined, cone-shaped cavity. The result is a detonation wave that subjects the liner to extreme pressure and heat, turning part of it into a jet of gas and molten metal. The jet converges and then streams forward at 27,000 feet per second, followed by a slower-moving slug formed from the remainder of the cone.

Portable and yet highly lethal, a Bofors, Infantry, Light and Lethal (BILL) antitank missile blasts out of its tripod-mounted launch tube *(far left)*. In an instant, narrow fins and rudders spring from the tail section, allowing the wire-guided infantry weapon to be steered until its sophisticated proximity sensor detects the target and detonates a shaped charge close above it. Designed to penetrate the light armor protecting the top of a tank's hull or turret, the BILL carries an unusual 100-mm warhead *(above)* that is tilted down at a thirty-degree angle, permitting the missile to attack from level flight.

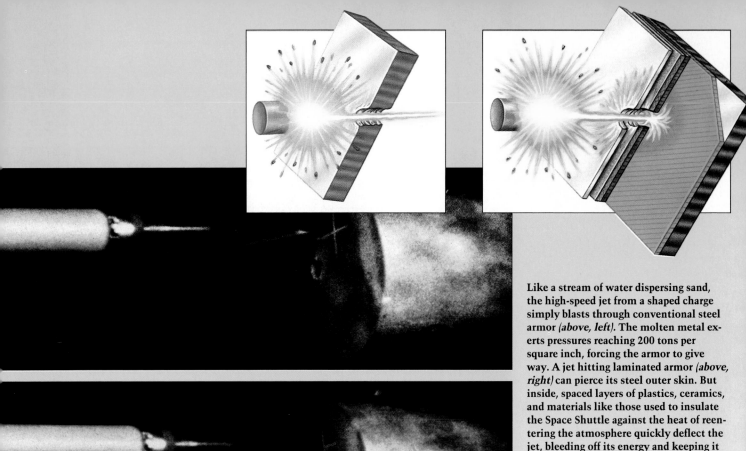

Like a stream of water dispersing sand, the high-speed jet from a shaped charge simply blasts through conventional steel armor *(above, left)*. The molten metal exerts pressures reaching 200 tons per square inch, forcing the armor to give way. A jet hitting laminated armor *(above, right)* can pierce its steel outer skin. But inside, spaced layers of plastics, ceramics, and materials like those used to insulate the Space Shuttle against the heat of reentering the atmosphere quickly deflect the jet, bleeding off its energy and keeping it from reaching the tank's interior.

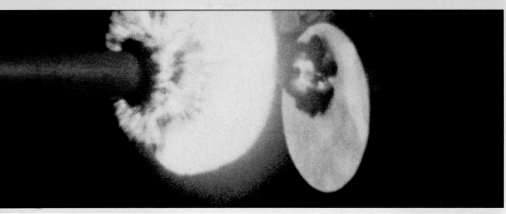

At the top of this four-picture sequence, a rocket-propelled HEAT warhead is milliseconds from delivering a devastating blow to its target—an *X* chalked on the end of a solid-steel rod. These photographs, taken at 8,000 frames a second, record the moment of impact. As the tip of the warhead strikes the rod, the shaped charge inside detonates with an expanding doughnut of white-hot gas. The explosion occurs several inches from the mark—optimum distance for the resulting jet, which then bores into the steel easily. In the bottom frame, the explosion engulfs the rod.

...k Armor That Fights Fire with Fire

Tanks not protected with Chobham-type laminated armor still stand a good chance of defeating HEAT warheads if they wear a suit of so-called reactive armor. First deployed on Israeli M48, M60, and Centurion tanks in Lebanon during the summer of 1982, reactive armor counters shaped charges by exploding. The detonation disperses the destructive high-speed jet before it can begin to penetrate.

Reactive armor consists of custom-made panels fastened to a tank's main armor. Each one contains an explosive charge that disregards small-arms fire, mortar and artillery fragments, extreme temperatures, and other battlefield tortures but detonates on contact with an incoming shaped-charge warhead, spewing blast and steel bits into the jet's path.

Five times more effective against shaped charges than conventional armor, panels like those fastened to the turret and elsewhere on the Israeli M60 shown below afford welcome protection, especially against top-attack weapons. But they do not interfere with the tank's guns, optics, or escape hatches, nor do they significantly decrease its mobility. Nonetheless, reactive armor is not invincible: Each panel explodes only once, exposing the armor beneath it to follow-up attacks.

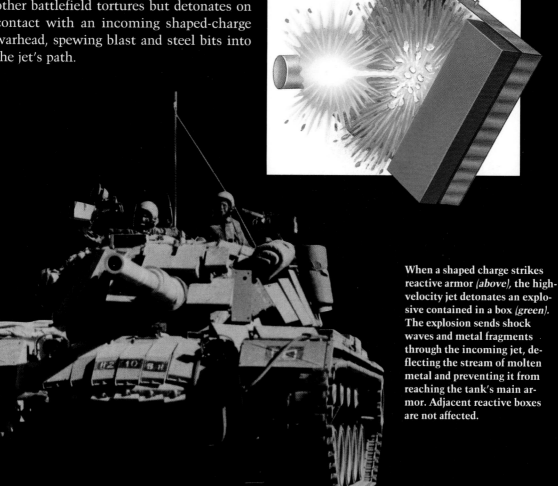

When a shaped charge strikes reactive armor *(above)*, the high-velocity jet detonates an explosive contained in a box *(green)*. The explosion sends shock waves and metal fragments through the incoming jet, deflecting the stream of molten metal and preventing it from reaching the tank's main armor. Adjacent reactive boxes are not affected.

3

Modern Battlefield Heavyweights

In the Yom Kippur War of 1973, tanks on both sides of the battle had to come to a full halt before the main gun was fired if the crew hoped for a good chance of a hit with the first shot. It had always been clear that if a tank could fire accurately at speed, especially against a moving target, it not only could kill enemy tanks more efficiently but would probably avoid being struck longer than a tank that had to stop to shoot. Thus, many tanks of that era and before had turret-stabilization systems that made some provision for keeping a gun trained on a target while on the move. But not until the advent of modern computerized stabilization systems could moving tanks fire accurately at moving targets.

Less than a decade after Israel's defense of the Golan Heights against the Syrians and the defeat of Egypt in the Sinai, a new generation of main battle tanks has made the main battle tanks of the 1970s seem antiquated. Firing accurately while under way is an option in most of these new, so-called third-generation vehicles. Armor has been toughened to better withstand new and more powerful antitank munitions. Guns have been enlarged for greater deadliness, and safety for the crew has been improved. With few exceptions, the new tanks are quicker to accelerate and faster at top speed than their predecessors. From Soviet designers have come the T-72 and the T-80, and an even more modern tank has been reported. Israel has assembled a force of Merkava tanks of its own design and manufacture. Britain has the Challenger, and Germany equips its army with the Leopard II. France will shortly field its LeClerc, and in the M1 Abrams, the United States has a tank that many authorities on armor view as the premier example of the age.

Many things separate the M1 from its predecessor, a main battle tank (MBT) called the M60. Depending on the model, the Abrams weighs as much as eight tons more than the older vehicle. In its more advanced models, it has a main gun of larger caliber for greater range and striking power. Its armor is of tough composite construction, made with layers of different materials that together are much more effective than the strongest steel at stopping antitank munitions. Moreover, the power plant is not the traditional diesel piston engine that moves most MBTs. Instead, the Abrams has a gas-turbine engine capable of producing 1,500 horsepower at full throttle—enough to accelerate the tank to twenty miles per hour in about six seconds and to propel it at a top speed of forty-five miles per hour. Emitting a sound like a huge vacuum cleaner, the M1 is quiet compared with most diesel-powered MBTs, and its exhaust is smokeless.

Speed and silence can be used to great advantage on the battlefield. In 1982, during a NATO training exercise in Germany, a battalion of fifty-eight American M1s surprised a column of Canadian-manned Leopard tanks acting as stand-ins for their Warsaw Pact counterparts. The Abrams battalion opened fire, and before the Canadians could respond, every one of their MBTs and APCs had been judged put out of action by exercise umpires. Later, an "enemy" officer, astonished at the swiftness and finality of the action, would say of his ambush by M1s: "One minute it's quiet, with no contact. The next minute you are overwhelmed, swarmed with quick, whispering death." Similar results in other exercises lead many American tank commanders to believe that the Abrams will have the same effect in actual combat.

Even if only an exercise, that battle in Germany was an impressive demonstration of the M1—intended to be the heart of U.S. armored forces well into the next millennium. The outcome would very likely have been the same had the encounter occurred in nighttime darkness or pea-soup fog or amid the man-made murk of a defensive smoke screen. So effective are the viewing systems of

the Abrams main battle tank—and so superior to those of any potential opponent—that low visibility is deemed a plus by its crews. The old army adage that "real battles only take place at night, in the rain, uphill, and at the intersection of four map sheets" has, with the M1, lost most of its bite.

Perhaps even more remarkable than the M1's stealthiness and round-the-clock, all-weather combat potential is its fire-control system. Coordinated by a computer buried in the turret, it considers atmospheric conditions, the type of ammunition and its temperature in the magazine, wear the gun barrel has seen, and other factors. Then the computer applies the data to a range obtained by timing the round trip of a pulse of laser light to the target, and elevating the gun and bringing it to bear on the quarry. For distances up to 4,400 meters, the probability of a hit with some kinds of ammunition on the first shot is better than 90 percent.

A skilled gunner in an M60 could shoot with similar accuracy to about 2,200 yards—as long as he and his target were stationary. But if an enemy tank was in motion, the probability of a hit for an M60 gunner could drop to less than 50 percent, whereas an M1 gunner remains almost certain of success, as he does if the Abrams is also under way. Arranging for the M1's main armament to track a moving target as its own platform bounds across field and stream is a technological tour de force. It depends for success not only on accurate ranging by laser, but also on a supple suspension, an electrically operated hydraulic system to stabilize the gun, and the tank's fire-control computer.

Potent, agile, and brimming with sophisticated electronics, the M1 Abrams may well be the greatest fighting machine on land—for the American vision of armored warfare at least. This vision is known as the air-land battle, and it features a high degree of mobility on the ground, highly accurate, fast-firing weapons systems, and maneuver tactics designed to seize the initiative from the enemy. The British, Germans, and French share this view to a large degree, and their MBTs, although they differ in details, are actually quite similar to one another in concept and capabilities. Indeed, most tanks around the world are more alike than they are different. Because they all must accomplish substantially the same missions, they must be mobile, have adequate firepower, and ideally be tough enough to absorb a good deal of punishment on the battlefield from a variety of threats ranging from other tanks and artillery to fast-moving fighter-bombers, tank-hunting helicopters, antitank guided missile teams, and even solitary infantrymen armed with simple, unguided rockets.

Punctuating the similarities, however, are significant differences, the result of nations' extrapolating from experience toward a plan for using tanks in the future. The Soviets, for example, have always intended to inundate the battlefield with masses of MBTs to overwhelm even the most technologically advanced defense. This philosophy has led to designs that have tended to emphasize rugged simplicity over technological sophistication. Israel, after thoroughly analyzing the trials of battles with her neighbors, developed the Merkava, which to some extent subordinates speed to firepower, survivability, and safety for the crew. Sweden, planning only to repel invaders, invented the S-tank. This turretless, rapid-firing MBT standing only six feet tall excels at point defense but might fare less well on the attack.

Nowhere is the solemn game of measure against countermeasure—of science and engineering applied to enhance the deadliness of men and machines and, simultaneously, to sweep them from the battlefield—played more earnestly than in the realm of the main battle tank. After the first day or two of the Yom Kippur War, the tank was widely said to have been made obsolete by improvements in weapons designed to kill it—primarily antitank guided missiles. Careful examination, however, revealed that improved tactics as well as advanced technology could alleviate the problems, and today, the main battle tank remains a commanding presence on the battlefield and the cutting edge of modern land warfare.

Main Battle Tanks of the Third Generation

The capabilities of any tank can be summed up in three terms: mobility, lethality, and survivability. The three characteristics are interrelated—part of a single equation. Thick armor, for example, is an important factor in a tank's ability to endure punishment on the battlefield and keep on fighting. But the stuff is staggeringly heavy, and while bulk may permit a bigger, more powerful gun, the added weight can also slow the vehicle and bog it down in soil that might support a lighter tank. Such penalties in mobility then become factors in survivability. Long live the tank that can dash agilely across a battlefield, either to spoil the aim of an enemy tank gunner or, by reaching cover, to elude a guided missile. And long live the tank that can shoot sooner, more accurately, and with a more devastating round than the opponent.

Since stretching a tank's capacity in one direction usually shortens it in others, tank designs are almost always compromises that sacrifice a little of this for a little of that to make a weapons system that is as well suited as possible to the battles it is expected to fight.

The United States, which has long enjoyed a reputation as a leader in the design of missiles and aircraft, has not, until recently, mastered the art of the trade-off in tank design. Although the Grants and Shermans of the Second World War were tough, they were outclassed by Germany's Tigers and Panthers. Victory came from superior numbers rather than first-rate weapons.

A decade later, confronting the Soviet Union in a protracted cold war, U.S. military leaders found numbers working against them. Each year, the Russians produced some 2,750 main battle tanks for themselves and many others for client states. U.S. output was perhaps less than a quarter of that, and its then-current main battle tank, the M48, could claim no more than equality with the Soviet T-55, then just beginning to enter service. Nor did the M60—a new

American tank with thicker armor than the M48's, a bigger gun, and improved gunsights, which was scheduled to enter production in the early 1960s—seem likely to compensate for vastly superior numbers of Soviet MBTs.

In 1963, concluding that an entirely new main battle tank was needed, the U.S. Army entered into a joint program with West Germany to develop the new weapon, known as the MBT70. The partnership made sense; identical tanks would simplify the logistics of any defense of Germany against an attack from the east. The MBT70 was an ambitious project. Plans called for the new tank to have, among other features, a laser range finder for accurately gauging target distance, innovative turret stabilization for firing while on the move, a sensitive television viewing system for night fighting, machinery to load the main gun automatically, and air conditioning for the crew.

By 1967, German and American prototypes had been built, but in the meantime, a new kind of armor had been invented in Britain by Gilbert Harvey. Instead of using steel exclusively, Harvey combined layers of various materials, including plastics and ceramics. He carefully spaced the laminations to defeat the high-velocity jet from a variety of antitank warhead, called a shaped charge *(pages 72-73)*, that allowed a courageous infantryman or antitank guided missile team to stand up to a tank and threatened the battlefield supremacy of armor. Harvey's invention, known as Chobham armor for the laboratory where it was developed, promised to restore the tank to its former pinnacle.

However, to incorporate Chobham armor in the MBT70 would have meant redesigning the tank, which was already being criticized not only for development costs and future operating expenses, but also for its complexity, thought beyond the ken of the average GI. In January 1971, the two allies decided to abandon the MBT70 and go their separate ways. The German way led to the Leopard II, the American way to the M1 Abrams, named for General Creighton Abrams, a cigar-chewing World War II tank hero. On February 28, 1980, nine years after the demise of the MBT70, the first production Abrams tanks were delivered to the U.S. Army. By the end of the decade, the Army would have nearly 7,000 of the 8,000 ordered in two versions—the original M1 and the heavier M1A1, which has a bigger gun, better armor, and superior protection for the crew against radioactive fallout and chemical and biological weapons.

Bursting onto the scene in 1980 with tough Chobham-style armor *(pages 66-67)*, a powerful gas-turbine engine, better acceleration than any of its contemporaries, and the ability to fire accurately on the move, the M1 Abrams main battle tank gave the U.S. Army perhaps the world's most formidable land weapon. But even before the M1 entered production, the Army saw that it could be substantially improved.

The tank's 105-mm main gun, puny in comparison to the 120-mm cannon in Germany's Leopard series, for example, made it impossible for German and American units in NATO to share ammunition. So the Army decided to fit the M1 with the German gun, which imparts nearly 30 percent more energy to a penetrator round, greatly improving armor penetration.

Another shortcoming was the lack of protection against nuclear, chemical, or biological attack. The solution was to add an air-conditioning and ventilation system. It supplies cool air to vests worn by the crew and breathable air to face masks. The system also keeps the air pressure inside the tank high enough to prevent contaminants from entering through joints or seams.

The new model, which also incorporated stronger armor and other, minor improvements was introduced in the mid-1980s as the M1A1.

A prototype of another Abrams upgrade, the M1A2, began tests in 1990 *(below)*. This latest—and possibly final—version adds a new so-called hunter-killer capability: While the gunner fires at one target through his thermal imaging system, the commander can use another viewer to point out the next target to the tank's fire-control system. Combined with other advances, the hunter-killer option will keep the M1 series in the front rank of the world's tanks until well into the next century.

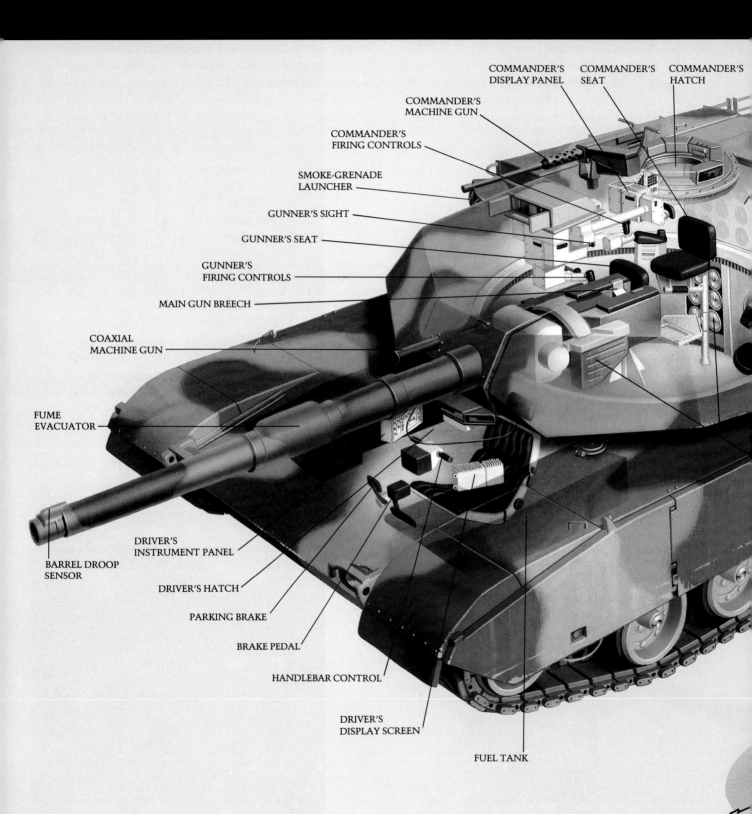

COMMANDER'S
DISPLAY PANEL

COMMANDER'S
SEAT

COMMANDER'S
HATCH

COMMANDER'S
MACHINE GUN

COMMANDER'S
FIRING CONTROLS

SMOKE-GRENADE
LAUNCHER

GUNNER'S SIGHT

GUNNER'S SEAT

GUNNER'S
FIRING CONTROLS

MAIN GUN BREECH

COAXIAL
MACHINE GUN

FUME
EVACUATOR

DRIVER'S
INSTRUMENT PANEL

DRIVER'S HATCH

BARREL DROOP
SENSOR

PARKING BRAKE

BRAKE PEDAL

HANDLEBAR CONTROL

DRIVER'S
DISPLAY SCREEN

FUEL TANK

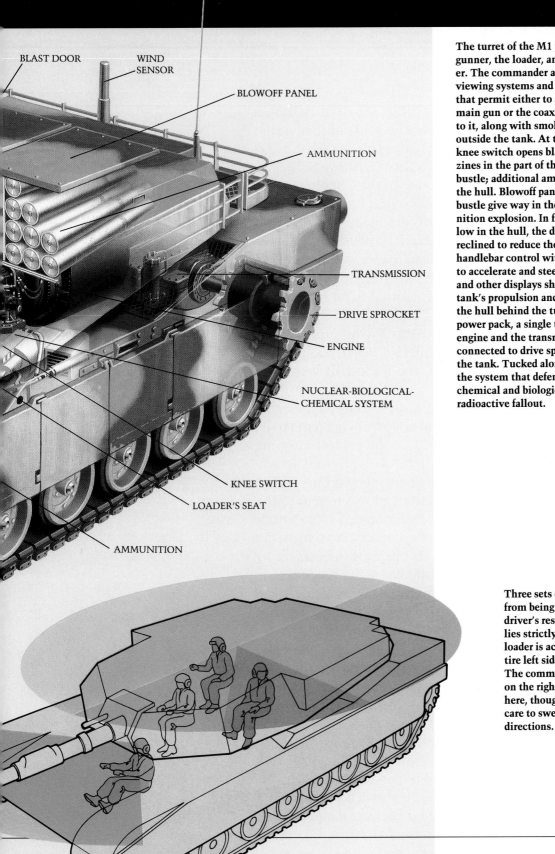

BLAST DOOR

WIND SENSOR

BLOWOFF PANEL

AMMUNITION

TRANSMISSION

DRIVE SPROCKET

ENGINE

NUCLEAR-BIOLOGICAL-CHEMICAL SYSTEM

KNEE SWITCH

LOADER'S SEAT

AMMUNITION

The turret of the M1 provides seats for the gunner, the loader, and the tank commander. The commander and the gunner have viewing systems and duplicate controls that permit either to aim and fire the main gun or the coaxial machine gun next to it, along with smoke-grenade launchers outside the tank. At the loader's station, a knee switch opens blast doors to magazines in the part of the turret called the bustle; additional ammunition is stored in the hull. Blowoff panels in the top of the bustle give way in the event of an ammunition explosion. In front of the turret, low in the hull, the driver sits almost fully reclined to reduce the height of the hull. A handlebar control with a throttle is used to accelerate and steer, while instruments and other displays show the status of the tank's propulsion and drive systems. In the hull behind the turret lies the tank's power pack, a single unit comprising the engine and the transmission, which is connected to drive sprockets at the rear of the tank. Tucked alongside the turret is the system that defends the tank against chemical and biological agents—as well as radioactive fallout.

Three sets of eyes keep the M1 from being caught off guard. The driver's responsibility *(green)* lies strictly forward, but the loader is accountable for the entire left side of the tank *(red)*. The commander concentrates on the right side, as shown here, though he generally takes care to sweep his gaze in all directions.

M1. The very designation promised a fresh start rather than a refinement of the M60, and nowhere was the spirit of innovation more evident than in the new tank's power plant. At least 1,200 horsepower was needed to move the M1's fifty-eight-ton bulk. Perhaps six tons of the weight was attributable to the Chobham-style armor. A diesel engine offered proven technology, but the weight of a twelve-cylinder model would have been prodigious.

Instead, M1 designers turned to the aviation industry for an air-cooled gas-turbine engine called a turboshaft and used in helicopters, where reliability and light weight are essential. These hallmarks of aircraft engines are almost as important to tank designers as they are to aeronautical engineers. The engine chosen was a 1,500-hp model built for helicopters by Avco Lycoming and modified by the company for installation in an MBT. Besides being a ton lighter than a diesel of the same power, the turboshaft was more compact than a diesel and, pound for pound, significantly more powerful. A gas turbine is quieter than a diesel and produces an exhaust that is less sooty. It has one-third fewer moving parts to be maintained or replaced. It starts instantly on the coldest morning and needs no time to warm up.

The quickness afforded by the turboshaft engine was impressive, even thrilling. In the fall of 1979, four of the tanks were sent to the Armor Center at Fort Knox, Kentucky, and assigned to an armor platoon. The intent was to see if the new machine was, in Army parlance, GI-proof—that is, if it could be operated effectively by soldiers rather than by the technicians who had so far been its only crews. (A rueful saying of General Abrams himself: If you leave the average soldier alone in the desert with an anvil for two or three days, the anvil will end up broken.) Shortly after the arrival of the tanks, the executive officer of the platoon's parent unit, Major David Owen, received a radio summons from the military police to a hard-packed dirt road leading to a tank training range. When he arrived, he found two of his crews detained, charged with speeding.

According to the arresting MPs, still unhappily layered in the talcum-fine dust thrown up by the tanks, the Abrams had been clocked in a speed trap—set up to snare overeager soldiers heading for home—doing better than fifty miles per hour in a thirty-five-mph zone. The eighteen- to twenty-one-year-old GIs had felt a need to see what a vehicle with a 1,500-hp engine (unequipped as yet with the governor that would limit the M1's speed to about forty-five miles per hour) could do. Citing the rooster tail of dust stirred up behind them and the noise inside the tank, the unrepentant young tankers protested they had not seen the MPs' flashing lights or heard their sirens until they stopped at the gunnery range that was their destination. Instead of confining the soldiers to barracks, Major Owen gave them a stern lecture and offered the MPs a ride in the tank. And there the matter ended.

Despite the advantages, a gas-turbine engine appeared in only one other third-generation tank design—the Soviet T-80. All other nations—Germany with the Leopard II, Britain with its Challenger, and Israel with its Merkava, for example—use diesel engines in their tanks. One reason is that a turbine engine requires three times as much air as a diesel of comparable horsepower, and the air must be kept scrupulously clean—a considerable challenge on a battlefield replete with dust, dirt, and grit. High-capacity, readily replaceable air filters would be a necessity. And they had to seat perfectly; poor fit of filters on early test models allowed grit to enter, ruining engines in one-tenth their expected service lives. The problem was quickly solved, though desert conditions can require changing or cleaning filters two or three times a day.

A more intractable problem is the thirst of a turbine engine for fuel. At full throttle, the M1 burns nearly four gallons per mile, while the Leopard's equally powerful diesel consumes only three gallons per mile. For much of an MBT's combat day, however, the engine is idling as tanks wait, primed for action. At such times a diesel engine conserves fuel, while a turbine burns fuel at almost the same rate as it does when charging forward. Thus the overall fuel efficiency of the Abrams could well be less than three-quarters that of the Leopard. In combat, a single M1 could guzzle up to 500 gallons a day; a division of 360 Abrams would burn 180,000 gallons of fuel for its tanks alone. To carry this daily fuel draft would require twenty tank trucks, "lucrative targets" in the words of fighter pilots. A division of 360 Leopard tanks would need only fifteen.

For these and other reasons, leaders of American armored force initially had little enthusiasm for an MBT with a turbine engine, and many continue to be concerned. Nothing except running out of bullets, perhaps, is more frustrating or more threatening to a tank unit than running out of gas. However, the reliability of the turbine engine has indirectly compensated somewhat for the increased concern about fuel supply.

Israel's Chariot of Firepower

Few weapons better reflect the political and social ideas of the country that built them than the Merkava, or Chariot, the main battle tank introduced by Israel in 1978. The first tank designed and manufactured in Israel, the Merkava met a major political need—independence from sometimes fickle foreign suppliers. But even more important was the survival of the crew. From the first line laid down on the drawing board, the Merkava was created to provide the best protection possible for the men inside.

The driving force behind development of the new tank was Major General Israel Tal, a hero of the Six-Day War and commander of the armored corps from 1964 to 1969. Tal was deeply affected by the heavy losses among tank crews in the early days of the Yom Kippur War of 1973, and he determined to push for a new Israeli tank designed to emphasize crew survivability.

Designers positioned the crew in the rear center of the tank and surrounded them with armor. Construction followed a "spaced armor" principle, with every component of the Merkava—power plant, ammunition, fuel, hydraulic lines—sited within armor-plated compartments that would absorb or weaken the effects of blast, heat, fire, and shrapnel. Placing the engine in front of the tank added a massive bulwark at the vehicle's most exposed spot. It also made possible a wide rear door in the fighting compartment. This opening permitted quick exit in an emergency and rapid refilling of ammunition magazines. Through this door the Merkava could also load as many as four infantrymen for an attack or pick up wounded troops in battle.

During Israel's 1982 invasion of southern Lebanon, not one Merkava crewman was killed, despite frequent PLO guerrilla ambushes and set-piece battles with Syrian tanks.

General Israel Tal, father of the Merkava, was a tanker's tanker. Even as the commander of Israel's armored corps, he regularly visited the firing range to preserve his reputation as the corps' best gunner.

A tank's power plant is only the starting point of mobility. To advance or retreat, attack or defend, a tank must be able to traverse all kinds of difficult country—steep grades, ditches, forests, sand, or boggy tundra. It must be able to maneuver through narrow city streets with right-angle intersections, just as it must also stop quickly, back up rapidly, and turn on a dime. The source of this versatility is the tank's running gear—its tracks and suspension.

A tank moves by rolling along a roadway of track. Built somewhat like bicycle chains, tracks are driven by sprockets at the rear of the tank, which are connected to the engine through a transmission. To advance the vehicle, for example, the sprockets turn so that they pick up links of track after the tank has passed by and shuttle them forward to lay on the ground ahead of the vehicle.

In response to this action, the tank rolls forward on wheels called road wheels, usually six or seven per side. Each road wheel turns on an axle that is linked to the tank's hull by a spring. Together, the springs support the weight of the tank and cushion the ride, just as they do in an automobile suspension. Many tanks, including the M1, the Leopard, and some Soviet models, use the springiness obtained from twisting a steel rod. In one version of this arrangement, called a torsion-bar suspension, the road-wheel axle is attached to an arm that is clamped around the end of the rod, which twists as the road wheel bobs over rough ground. To control the bouncing road wheels, tanks use shock absorbers. However, instead of telescoping hydraulic units like those found on cars, the M1 uses rotary hydraulic shocks.

The width of an MBT's tracks and the length in contact with the ground as the tank rolls along are important to mobility because, relative to the weight of the tank, they determine the so-called footprint pressure the tank exerts on the ground. If the pressure is too great, the tank may become mired in mud or break through bridge decking or lightly paved roads. The sixty-three-ton M1A1, standing on tracks twenty-five inches wide that stretch fifteen feet along the ground, has a footprint pressure of fourteen pounds per square inch, which is fairly typical of third-generation MBTs. By comparison, the average 150-pound infantryman weighed down with sixty pounds of combat gear has about the same footprint pressure. Even so, an M1 cannot tag along everywhere a soldier can walk; though the soil may support a soldier, it might not withstand the grinding of a tank's tracks.

ISRAELI MERKAVA

The Merkava's creators departed from accepted tank doctrine in settling for a low top speed—twenty-eight miles per hour—in favor of heavy armor and better crew protection. Put to the test in the 1982 Israeli incursion into Lebanon, the tank proved capable of effective action even in the close confines of city streets.

BRITISH CHALLENGER

Thickly clad in British-developed Chobham composite armor, the sixty-one-ton Challenger nevertheless enjoys a 50 percent better power-to-weight ratio than its much lighter predecessor, the Chieftain, thanks to its 1,200-hp V-twelve Rolls-Royce engine.

U.S. M1 ABRAMS

The first MBT to use a turbine engine, the Abrams overcame early mechanical problems and critical media attention to establish a reputation as the most reliable, easy-to-maintain tank ever made.

GERMAN LEOPARD II

Developed after the failure of a joint German-U.S. MBT project, the Leopard II came into service in 1979, pioneering the 120-mm gun that was later fitted to the Abrams. Although the Leopard II weighs sixty tons, its ten-cylinder diesel engine can propel it to a road speed of forty-five miles per hour.

FRENCH LECLERC

The LeClerc has a highly compact 1,500-hp turbocharged diesel engine. Its automatic-loading main gun can fire fifteen rounds per minute while on the move. Detachable armor allows for quick battlefield repairs and inexpensive upgrading to exploit advances in armor technology.

SOVIET T-72

The T-72 evolved from earlier models dating all the way back to World War II. It features a low silhouette, a hard-to-penetrate mushroom-shaped turret, and a 125-mm main gun with an automatic loader. It carries a crew of three—one fewer than most other MBTs—and at forty-five tons is far lighter than its Western counterparts.

Along with traversing rough ground and maneuvering in tight quarters, main battle tanks must be able to cross water barriers such as streams and rivers. The M1A1 and most other late-model tanks can ford streams up to four feet deep, provided the bottom is firm, by simply closing off drains in the bottom of the hull. That depth can be doubled by rigging a snorkel, a vertical tube that enables the engine to receive the air it needs for combustion.

Touring the countryside, of course, is only incidental to a main battle tank's role as a machine of destruction. As General George S. Patton, Jr., famed for his aggressive command of armored forces in the Second World War, said, exhorting his tankers: "Cut through and end up in the rear. Then do something, goddamn it, do something!" For the most part, the something he had in mind was done with the tank's main gun.

The firing of a tank cannon is like nothing else in modern warfare. It is most akin to the firing of naval turret guns but takes place in a far more confined and crowded space. In the M1A1, for example, the gun's breech recoils between the gunner and loader, shooting back like a horizontal pile driver acting with a force exceeding 100 tons. Buttoned up inside the tank, their ears clamped between headphones for the intercom and radios, the crew feels a lurch, hardly noticing the gun's report. As the gun tube moves forward in counterrecoil, the breech snaps open and ejects a hot stub of shell casing into a container on the deck; most of the casing, being combustible, burns when the weapon discharges. A powerful fan whirs on to expel gun smoke from the turret and bore, but the ventilating action is never perfect, and the tank interior is tainted with an acrid, penetrating odor of cordite fumes—an aphrodisiac to a true tanker, says one of the breed. The loader turns, pulls another fifty-five-pound round from the ammo rack, and slams it into the open breech for the next shot.

The destructive power of any gun depends largely on the diameter of its bore—usually measured in millimeters—and the propulsive force from rapidly expanding gases of the ignited propellant. The larger the caliber, the bigger the projectile that can be delivered to the target. And, of course, the more powerful the charge, the more energy it imparts to the projectile while it is in the barrel.

Like the power of its engine, the bore of the tank's main gun has

Hydropneumatic suspension—using compressed fluid and air to damp wheel bounce—may offer more road-holding capability for tanks than the traditional torsion bars and shock absorbers. It enables tanks like the French LeClerc, shown here, to keep most road wheels on the ground while surmounting a sharp bump.

increased over the years, from the 76 millimeters of late-model Shermans from World War II to the 90 millimeters of the 1950s-era M48; the 105-mm weapon of the M60, the M1, and Israel's early Merkavas to the 120-mm cannon of the M1A1, the Leopard II, the British Challenger, the French LeClerc, and the Merkava III. The Soviets, in their T-72 and T-80 tanks, have turned to a 125-mm cannon. But caliber cannot be increased without limit. Larger shells take up more room, reducing the number of rounds that a tank can carry in the space allotted to magazines. Larger guns are heavier than smaller ones, too, and require a heavier tank to withstand the increased recoil.

The M1A1's main gun and those of most of its peers are smoothbore—without spiral rifling grooves that spin and stabilize a projectile in the same way that a quarterback imparts a stabilizing spin to a football. However, spinning helps neither munition commonly fired by the main gun. Rod penetrators *(page 68)*, which punch through armor by virtue of mass and speeds that can exceed a mile a second, are so long compared to their diameter that they tend to become unstable if spun in flight. High-explosive antitank (HEAT) rounds pierce armor with a high-velocity jet of molten metal moving at 18,000 miles per hour or more *(pages 72-73)*. Centrifugal forces that result from spinning deform the jet enough to diminish its effectiveness by half. In smoothbore guns especially, both rounds are stabilized by fins.

The fire-control systems that aim the guns of today's main battle tanks are marvels of electronic wizardry. Virtually all of the newest MBTs have viewing and sighting systems that let the crew carry on the battle through darkness by amplifying the faint light from stars, the moon, or other sources. Other instruments, called thermal imaging systems (TIS), can pierce rain, smoke, fog, or camouflage by sensing infrared radiation emitted even by cold targets. This feat is accomplished by using a detector held at − 320 degrees Fahrenheit. Anything on the battlefield, even if it is above the Arctic Circle in winter, will appear warm to a TIS.

One U.S. Army lieutenant colonel with a twenty-year career in armor described his first experience with the thermal imaging system of the Abrams in tones of awe. "The fog was so thick," he said of attempting to pierce the mist with his own eyes, "that other tanks less than fifty meters away were completely invisible." Then he looked through the TIS. "There they were in black and white and gray," he marveled, "with the heads and shoulders of the commanders and their loaders plainly visible. Up ahead, more than two miles away, were a couple of water tanks. Not only could I see them clearly, but I could easily discern the level of the water in them." Because of heat in the water, the tanks were warmer near the bottoms than at the tops.

Once the gunner in a modern tank has identified a target, he takes aim with a gunsight that uses a laser range finder to gauge target distance within a few yards. A computer takes into account more than a dozen factors that influence the flight of a projectile, then lays the gun accordingly. At ranges of a mile and more, depending on terrain and atmospheric conditions, it is almost impossible to miss. Furthermore, the probability of a hit remains almost as high if both the tank and its target are moving.

There are several components to this steadiness of aim. First, the tank's turret must remain level to keep the gun from dipping and rising as the tank follows undulations of the terrain at speeds up to forty-five miles per hour. This is done by means of powerful electric motors and hydraulic pumps that rapidly compensate for hull tilt toward the front, rear, or either side. Next, the sighting system must determine where the target will be a second or two after the shot is fired in order not to miss to the rear. (At forty-five miles per hour, an M1 travels about three tank lengths in one second.) The data for this calculation comes from the gunner, who keeps the gunsight

A Singular Tank from Scandinavia

A nation intent on both fiercely defending its borders and not appearing belligerent to a mighty neighbor might well choose a tank much different from those built by the superpowers and their allies. Neutral Sweden is just such a state, and beginning in the late 1950s, this small Scandinavian country designed and produced a most unusual fighting machine—the Stridsvgn 103, or S-tank (above).

Most distinctive about the S-tank is the lack of a turret. Instead, the 105-mm main gun is fixed pointing straight forward. To swing the weapon toward a target, the gunner-driver turns the entire tank. Special gear ratios in the tank's transmission allow him to spin the tank as much as ninety degrees in a second to confront a threat or to adjust the aim as finely as he could a turret-mounted weapon.

To raise or lower the gun, the entire tank tilts by means of hydrogas suspension arms on the tank's road wheels. These devices, never before used on an operational tank, support the vehicle's weight by means of a piston acting against a bubble of highly compressed nitrogen that serves instead of a spring or torsion bar. Introducing hydraulic fluid between the pistons and bubbles of all the suspension units raises the tank; draining fluid lowers it. The gunner-driver of an S-tank, by extending the front hydrogas unit as far as it will go and fully retracting the rearmost unit, can elevate the gun as much as twelve degrees above the horizon. Lowering the front and raising the rear depresses the gun as much as ten degrees.

The fixed gun has significant limitations: It cannot be aimed as quickly as a turret-mounted weapon, and it can be fired accurately only when the tank is stationary. For these reasons, it is better suited for firing from prepared defensive positions than for mounting an armor assault.

But the S-tank approach also offers offsetting advantages. Lacking a turret, for example, the S-tank stands only six feet three inches tall—an extraordinarily low profile that makes the vehicle all the more difficult to see and hit. Hidden in a firing position, which it can dig for itself with a retractable bulldozer blade, the tank exposes less than sixteen inches of its upperworks to enemy gunners.

An immobile gun also makes possible a simple and reliable autoloader. Mounted behind the breech at the rear of the tank, the autoloader not only permits the tank to fire a shot every four seconds—about twice as fast as the crew of an M1 can fire—it also reduces the crew of the S-tank to three. Besides the gunner-driver, there is a tank commander and a man-of-all-work who can operate the tank in reverse; assist the commander with communications, help with reloading, fueling, and maintenance; and keep an eye on the functioning of the tank's various systems.

Like the Merkava, the S-tank has its power plant in the front, where it offers the crew additional protection from anti-tank weapons. Two engines are installed there, a fuel-efficient diesel for most operations and an American-made gas turbine for an extra burst of speed during combat.

centered on the target while the fire-control computer calculates the lead—how far ahead of the target to aim. After tracking the target for at least three seconds, the gunner presses a button that activates the laser range finder. Immediately, a ready symbol appears in the gunsight. To shoot, the gunner pulls the trigger.

However, before the round is fired, the fire-control system makes another check. When the computer lit the ready light, it drew a small, imaginary rectangle, called a coincidence window, around the point where the shot will pass. As the gunner tracks the target with the gunsight, the computer traverses the turret and raises or lowers the gun to keep the coincidence window positioned for a hit. But it cannot compensate for every bounce and jostle of both vehicles; gun and turret are too massive to move so quickly. Instead, the computer postpones firing until the position of the gunsight telegraphs that the target has reentered the coincidence window. If hunter and prey are both stopped, the time between pulling the trigger and the report of the gun is imperceptible. When both vehicles are moving, the delay may be as much as a second or two. Longer than that, and the computer extinguishes the ready light to begin calculating a new firing solution.

The nimbleness to elude enemy fire and the ability to shoot accurately and quickly—to strike before being struck—contribute much to the survivability of a main battle tank. Yet even the most inept and poorly equipped opponent will sometimes score. An MBT's first line of defense against a hit, of course, is its armor. Chobham armor has remarkably improved the survivability of modern tanks, especially against shaped-charge munitions. For added protection against larger HEAT warheads, which may well penetrate even Chobham armor, Israel developed a shield called reactive armor. These boxes of explosives—about a foot long, ten inches wide, and two or three inches thick—are fastened to the tank's exterior and detonate when struck by a HEAT round, disrupting the fiery jet that would otherwise pierce the tank *(page 75)*. Reactive armor might on occasion also defend against a rod penetrator, depending on whether the impact set off the explosive and the angle at which the projectile strikes. Israel was the first country to bolt reactive armor to its main battle tanks and other armored vehicles, but that is only one of many imaginative ways in which Israel has increased the survivability of its tanks. For example, the Merkava has the engine in the front of the tank expressly to help stop a round from reaching the crew compartment.

When armor fails, a hit on a tank need not be fatal to the crew. Historically, as many tankers have been injured by fire and secondary explosions in the turret as from metal fragments that accompany a hit. Here, too, the Merkava is noteworthy. Israel discovered that many tankers, having survived a hit, were killed or wounded as they escaped through hatches in the top. Consequently, the Merkava is designed with an exit in the rear.

To reduce the hazard of fire, fuel in the Merkava III is carried in armored compartments outside the tank. The turret is electrically rather than hydraulically operated; hydraulic fluid under high pressure atomizes when lines rupture and becomes explosively flammable. Moreover, the fuel tanks are armored, self-sealing, and insulated with ceramic material, and fuel lines run through armored channels. Despite such fire-prevention measures, the tank also has a fast-acting fire-suppression system, as do the M1 and other third-generation MBTs. Infrared sensors instantly detect a fire and loose a smothering cloud of nontoxic gases that extinguish the flames in a tenth of a second, giving the men inside a chance to escape.

No fire extinguisher can put out an ammunition fire; the propellant contains its own oxygen. Thus the Leopard, the M1, and other modern MBTs store ammunition in compartments separated from the crew by stout bulkheads. In the event of an explosion, weaker exterior panels give way, sparing the crew from immolation.

On the modern battlefield, the armor soldier has more to worry about than incoming explosive and penetrating rounds. He must be ready to deal with such unseen but deadly threats as nuclear fallout,

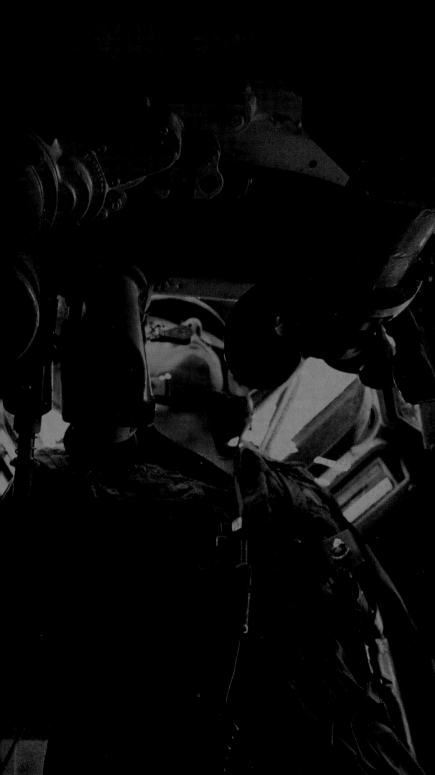

Teaming Up for Battle

To fight and prevail in war, the crew of an M1 tank—commander, gunner, loader, and driver—train hard to become a close-knit team, performing their separate but interdependent tasks in the tight confines of the crew compartment.

The driver monitors automotive systems and keeps the tank in running condition. In battle his duties are to look for any threats forward and to drive the smoothest route for accurate firing.

Maintaining and keeping count of the supply of shells for the main gun is the loader's responsibility. During a battle he responds instantly to the commander's call for ammunition, having a scant few seconds—while the gunner is aiming—to select and load the right shell.

The M1's precision fire-control instruments are under the gunner's care; he ensures that they are working and are properly calibrated. In battle he must keep his sight on the target, even at high speed over rough terrain. If the fire-control system fails, he must be able to aim and fire manually.

The commander is in charge of the tank and its crew. He has prime responsibility for spotting threats and for communicating with the crew and with other tanks in his unit. He gives all of the orders during a battle sequence.

What happens when the commander sees a target is revealed in the photographs on the following pages, taken during a live-fire exercise at Fort Carson, Colorado.

Standing in his hatch, an M1 commander looks for targets. If he sees an enemy tank, he will yell "Gunner! Sabot! Tank!" This notifies the gunner of the target's presence, tells the loader to insert a penetrator round in the gun, and describes the target.

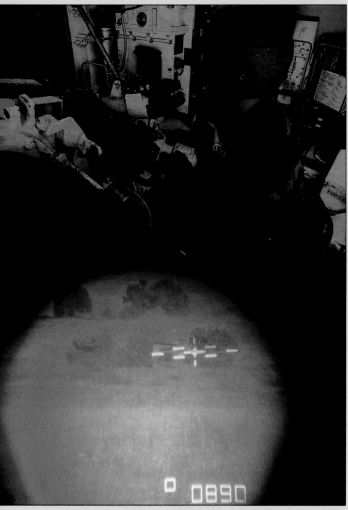

Alerted when the commander swings the main gun toward the enemy tank, the gunner looks for the target in his sight (*above, top*). When he has the reticle—the dot at the intersection of the cross hairs—squarely in the center of the target (*above, bottom*), he yells "Identified" and activates his laser range finder. Instantly, it calculates the distance to the target— 890 meters in this case— and displays it on the screen. The hollow square visible next to the range indicates that the loader has done his part and the gun is ready to fire.

In these pictures the action is taking place in daylight, and the sighting is optical. At night, or in smoke or fog, the gunner uses thermal imaging. Depending on his preference, the system shows the target as a black image on a white background—or vice versa.

Hearing the commander's call of "Sabot," the loader swivels his chair and hits the knee switch with his right knee, opening the ammunition door *(top left)*. He pulls out an armor-piercing, fin-stabilized, discarding-sabot cartridge *(top right)*, flips it 180 degrees while swiveling to the front *(above, left)*, and shoves the shell into the breech. After the breech automatically slams shut, the loader illuminates the ready-to-fire square in the gun-sight and yells, "Up!"

biological poisons, and chemical agents such as nerve and mustard gas. For protection, crewmen wear special clothing and face masks that supply filtered air. As extra insurance, cleansed air is also pumped into the crew compartment at a pressure exceeding that of the atmosphere outside, thus keeping airborne pollutants out.

Concern for crew survivability notwithstanding, a main battle tank is a dangerous place to be, the more so as tanks of potential adversaries adopt similar technologies. As in any fight where the equipment on both sides becomes about evenly matched, victory depends less on the weapons themselves than on the skills and spirit of the men doing the fighting.

The Soviet Breed of Tank

Soviet tanks—more than 60,000 in the Red Army and thousands more supplied to other nations—represent a philosophy quite different from the views that have shaped Western armor. The Soviet Union suffered 20 million killed in World War II. That nightmare left indelible scars on the national consciousness of the Soviet Union and gave added force to the perceived military lessons of the war. One lesson was paramount: Although the troopers of the Wehrmacht were better equipped, Luftwaffe planes superior, and some panzer divisions armed with more effective tanks, the preponderance of Russian numbers—the sheer, crushing weight of men and metal—brought victory in the end.

Nor, as the years passed, did the Russians forget the tank that brought them through their struggle for national survival—the T-34. They have never ceased to honor it. With only a few exceptions, all Soviet main battle tanks built since then have been derived from the T-34's basic design.

Ironically, the T-34 and its descendants got their start on the drawing board of an irascible American genius, J. Walter Christie. A none-too-successful designer, builder, and driver of racecars in the dawn years of the automobile, Christie produced his first tank in 1919. It was the earliest such vehicle to have a suspension. World War I tanks had been built without springs, dispensing bruises and even broken bones to their crews as they lurched across broken ground at five or six miles per hour. Speed was limited by the puny engines—eighty to ninety horsepower. Christie installed a 387-hp

Flaming gases erupt from the muzzle after the tank commander, upon hearing from the loader and gunner that the weapon is loaded and aimed, orders "Fire!" When the gunner hears the command, he responds "On the way," squeezing the trigger on the last word. The entire sequence—from sighting to firing—typically takes between five and eight seconds.

101

Liberty V-twelve aircraft engine in his tank, giving it a top speed of twenty-five miles per hour.

The 1919 tank also pioneered the use of large-diameter road wheels instead of a less supple suspension that the U.S. Army was experimenting with. Each road wheel actually consisted of two solid rubber wheels with a space between them. Cavities in the facing sides of these wheels accepted similarly shaped lugs in the center of the tank's tracks. This design allowed Christie to propel the tank with the road wheels instead of a sprocket. That, in turn, permitted the tank to operate without tracks, useful, thought the designer, for driving the tank to the front over paved roads. By 1927, the design had evolved into a truly remarkable machine. It had a turret with a 57-mm cannon and a .30-caliber machine gun, and it could travel at more than forty miles an hour across country on its tracks, and at seventy if the tracks were removed and the tank was driven on pavement.

At his own expense, Christie built several test models of the tank, intending to sell them to the U.S. Army. But a deal could not be struck before Christie, badly in need of cash, sold two of his creations to the Soviet Union, which began production of a Christie-type tank in 1930. The T-34, a successor that had lost the ability to travel trackless, entered service in 1940. In all, perhaps as many as 40,000 T-34s were built during the war.

Soviet armor tactics—steamrollering headlong into the opposition with overwhelming numbers—led to tanks quite different in some respects from American and European models, which since the mid-1970s have been designed expressly to counter such an attack. The typical Soviet tank has tended to be slower than its Western counterpart; speed is not essential where there is no intention to outmaneuver the opponent. Soviet armor advances in waves, firing on the move to keep the enemy's head down but without trying to shoot at individual targets. Consequently, Soviet designs have de-emphasized the quickly traversing turrets and advanced fire-control systems that their erstwhile enemies value so highly.

Soviet tanks have usually mounted bigger guns than their contemporaries in the West, yet they are also smaller in order to make them more difficult to hit as they advance on the foe. Compactness, however, has disadvantages, including the capacity to carry fewer

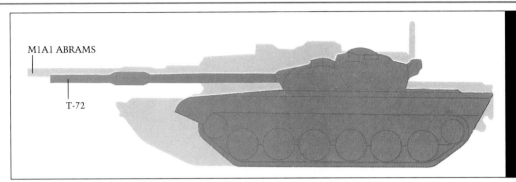

Compared to the M1 Abrams *(blue)*, the Soviet T-72 is smaller in every dimension. It reflects traditional Soviet armor doctrine: Overwhelm the enemy with mass formations of smaller, cheaper tanks. Only in the size of its main gun does the T-72 exceed the M1.

rounds for the main gun and cramped quarters for the crew. There is also no space for air-conditioning equipment. Heat in the crew compartment combines with high noise levels to fatigue the crew rapidly. Soviet tanks also tend to have ineffectual damage-control systems. Upon being hit, they are very likely to explode spectacularly in a pyrotechnic display that is almost always fatal to the crew.

For the most part, Soviet tanks show an evolutionary, step-by-step approach to design, in contrast to the start-from-scratch method that has produced some of the best Western tanks. For example, although the T-62 now in the field has a new 115-mm smoothbore gun, improved tracks, night-vision devices, and protection against toxic agents, the engine and transmission are basically the same as those introduced on the T-44 at the end of World War II and also used for the T-54 and T-55 that followed.

The T-72 continued the tradition of the Soviets' arming their tanks with ever-bigger guns. First paraded before the public in November of 1977, the tank has a 125-mm smoothbore cannon that fires a round consisting of two parts—a projectile and a powder charge. The gun is also served by a mechanical loader instead of a human one. "It is a great ram driven by hydraulics and compressed air," says retired general Donn Starry, an officer of more than thirty years' experience in armor. "It takes two 'chunk-chunks' of the ram to load each round, one for the warhead and one for the propellant and its casing. The ram moves with awesome force, directly past the gunner's right shoulder. Anything in the way gets rammed with terrific force."

The autoloader permits a reduction of the tank's crew from four to three. This in turn leads to a corresponding reduction of the armored volume inhabited by the crew and therefore a lower, less vulnerable tank—always an important goal in tank design. But the autoloader has some disadvantages: a slower rate of fire (the gun must be aligned with the loader after each shot); the inability to change the type of round once it has been loaded; the loss of a crew member who, besides loading, could help with such tasks as maintenance, refueling, and repair; and the addition of another complex, expensive mechanism subject to breakdown and malfunction.

The top-of-the-line Soviet tank is the T-80, introduced in 1979. Produced in two versions, it differs from earlier tanks in one important respect. Like the M1 Abrams, it has a gas-turbine engine, but the T-80's power plant generates about 1,000 horsepower. One variant of the T-80 has an improved autoloader. The other launches antitank guided missiles through the tube of its main armament; it, too, may have an autoloader. Some American tanks of the past have had the capability to launch antitank missiles, though the feature has fallen out of favor. Ammunition was expensive and slow-moving after launch, compared to gun projectiles. Moreover, maintenance of the complex fire-control systems needed to aim two entirely different varieties of munitions proved difficult, and the units were too often out of service.

The T-80's stabilized turret has a laser range finder, giving the tank substantially the same accuracy as the M1A1. Like all Soviet tanks, the T-80 is smaller, lighter, and lower than comparable Western MBTs—twenty tons lighter and seven inches lower than

Soviet T-72s with snorkels in place lumber ashore in a river-crossing exercise. The apparent independence from bridging equipment afforded by snorkels could prove illusory in combat. Rigging the snorkel and sealing the tank against leaks and then reversing the process after a crossing can take up to eight hours.

Britain's Challenger, thirteen tons lighter and nine inches lower than the Abrams, five tons lighter and almost two feet lower than the German Leopard II.

And like all new models of Soviet tanks, the T-80 is not a replacement of older versions, but an addition to the operational inventory. Soviet military planners still agree with Voltaire that "God is always for the big battalions," and it is rare indeed that they discard any weapons system that works. Thus a prospective Soviet opponent must expect to encounter many generations of main battle tanks, from the T-54 to the T-80. And an opponent can be sure of one other thing: Those tanks will advance in the hundreds or thousands—great masses of armor intended, as in battles fought half a century ago, to grind the enemy down.

The Tank Killers

Tanks advancing toward the forward line of troops, or FLOT, are a high-priority target. Much enemy effort is devoted to finding and destroying them before they can fire their guns. The number and variety of ways to accomplish this make the head spin: a heavily armed helicopter lurking behind a stand of trees, a jet fighter racing in behind the hill just ahead, other tanks that might have slipped through friendly forces, mines laid by special-operations troops or scattered along the line of march by artillery, helicopters, or close-support fighters. Any gully could hide a couple of men and a variety of missiles and rockets capable of disabling the tank and perhaps destroying it. Even with scouts to reconnoiter ahead and other means of averting surprise attack—battlefield radar and drones equipped with video cameras and other sensors, for example—no place is safe for a tank and its crew, no moment free of anxiety.

Besides being alert, the tank's best defense is to face the enemy; few munitions are capable of penetrating the vehicle's well-protected front. Armor for the M1 Abrams, for example, contains depleted uranium said to be capable of shielding the crew from even the most potent of HEAT warheads and rod penetrators, including the 125-mm projectiles fired by modern Soviet tanks. Where armor is thinner—top, bottom, sides, and rear—a tank is much more vulnerable, and those are the places where even a small antitank weapon can disable or even kill.

Prominent in the lethal array are lightweight rockets with shaped-charge warheads. Some of these can be carried and fired by one man. Perhaps best known of such weapons are the Soviet rocket-propelled grenades (RPGs). The grenade portion is a shaped charge; the rocket is a tube of propellant screwed into the back of the grenade. The package is slipped into a reusable launcher and fired by pulling a trigger. The Vietnam-vintage RPG-7 could blast through fifteen inches of plain armor, depending on the model. More modern RPG-18s and RPG-22s are fired from disposable launchers. A Swedish disposable called the AT-4 has been adopted by the U.S. Army to replace the Light Antitank Weapon (LAW). This American one-use rocket launcher, although it is effective against lightly armored vehicles such as personnel carriers, lacked the punch required to defeat a tank. The AT-4 can pierce almost eighteen inches of plain armor, more than protects most tanks except on the front.

No foot soldier would choose to go against a tank with either of these weapons or any like them, but their short range cuts two ways. To an infantryman 300 yards away, a tank can seem very close indeed. But a rocket from an AT-4, quickly reaching a speed of 650 miles per hour, covers the distance in just one second. Even if one of the tank crew sees the flash and smoke of the launch, there is little he can do besides warn the others with a call of "Missile!"

Weapons for use at greater distances give a tank more time to evade, so they are equipped with guidance systems that permit the missile to correct its course toward the target during flight. Joystick controls, such as the one used to guide the Soviet Sagger missile of Yom Kippur War vintage, have largely been abandoned in favor of optical guidance systems. Much simpler to use, such a system requires the missileer only to keep the cross hairs of a telescopic sight on the target as it moves. Doing so automatically sends appropriate instructions to the missile's steering vanes over wires that trail behind. There are many optically guided antitank guided missiles, or ATGMs, having maximum ranges between two and three miles: America's TOW (for tube-launched, optical-tracking, wire-guided), Sweden's BILL (page 73), the Soviet Spigot and Spandrel, and a European missile called HOT. The shoulder-fired BILL is the only such weapon light enough to be handled by an individual. Others can be deployed by a two- or three-man team but are also mounted on vehicles. The HOT is so heavy that a vehicle is essential.

During an exercise, crewmen load an M1 tank with dummy high-explosive antitank (HEAT) shells, which have canister-like projectiles *(above, right)* instead of the pointed penetrator of a kinetic energy round *(above, left)*. The job of refilling the forty-round magazines in an M1 armed with a 120-mm gun is strenuous work; each cartridge weighs more than fifty pounds.

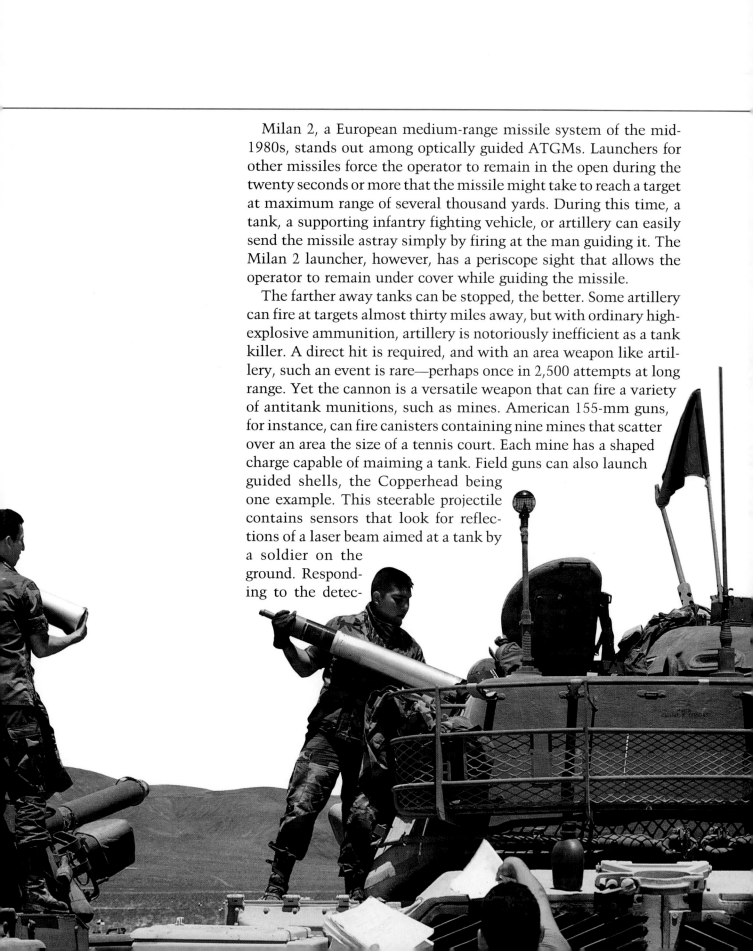

Milan 2, a European medium-range missile system of the mid-1980s, stands out among optically guided ATGMs. Launchers for other missiles force the operator to remain in the open during the twenty seconds or more that the missile might take to reach a target at maximum range of several thousand yards. During this time, a tank, a supporting infantry fighting vehicle, or artillery can easily send the missile astray simply by firing at the man guiding it. The Milan 2 launcher, however, has a periscope sight that allows the operator to remain under cover while guiding the missile.

The farther away tanks can be stopped, the better. Some artillery can fire at targets almost thirty miles away, but with ordinary high-explosive ammunition, artillery is notoriously inefficient as a tank killer. A direct hit is required, and with an area weapon like artillery, such an event is rare—perhaps once in 2,500 attempts at long range. Yet the cannon is a versatile weapon that can fire a variety of antitank munitions, such as mines. American 155-mm guns, for instance, can fire canisters containing nine mines that scatter over an area the size of a tennis court. Each mine has a shaped charge capable of maiming a tank. Field guns can also launch guided shells, the Copperhead being one example. This steerable projectile contains sensors that look for reflections of a laser beam aimed at a tank by a soldier on the ground. Respond-ing to the detec-

tion of laser radiation, a computer chip inside adjusts steering vanes, guiding the shell to a direct hit. In part because the man holding the laser is at risk with the Copperhead, new, autonomous munitions are under development. SADARM, for example *(pages 112-113)*, will be able to find and kill individual armored vehicles without human assistance.

All of the foregoing means of attacking tanks (except the tank itself) share the drawback that they must generally wait for targets to come to them. Aircraft are free of this shortcoming, and many types, helicopters and conventional aircraft alike, play antiarmor roles. Perhaps the most interesting of the fixed-wing tank killers are the A-10 Thunderbolt II and a Soviet copy called the Su-25 Frogfoot. The A-10, a heavily armed and armored twin-engine attack jet, is neither fast nor glamorous, but it is superbly maneuverable. It has four Maverick TV-guided missiles hung under the wings—plus a seven-barrel 30-mm cannon that spits out 4,200 depleted-uranium slugs per minute. An A-10 in the hands of a skilled pilot might well knock out several tanks before needing to rearm.

First fielded in the 1970s, the A-10 is an aging aircraft. It has a short range, cannot fight in bad weather or at night, and is good for only one thing—busting tanks. The U.S. Air Force plans to replace it with much faster planes such as the F-16 Falcon. Even though they would attack a tank flying little faster than an A-10, the added speed is necessary not so much to reach the battle in a shorter time as to get there at all, so serious is the threat from surface-to-air missiles and radar-directed antiaircraft guns.

Those who dispute these arguments contend that they are evidence of a low priority for battlefield air support among Air Force

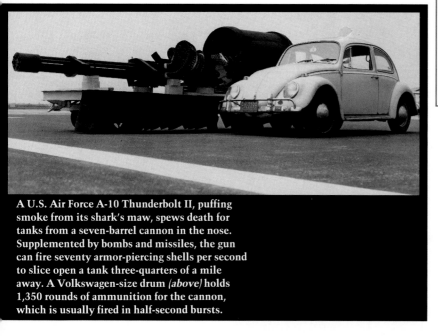

A U.S. Air Force A-10 Thunderbolt II, puffing smoke from its shark's maw, spews death for tanks from a seven-barrel cannon in the nose. Supplemented by bombs and missiles, the gun can fire seventy armor-piercing shells per second to slice open a tank three-quarters of a mile away. A Volkswagen-size drum *(above)* holds 1,350 rounds of ammunition for the cannon, which is usually fired in half-second bursts.

planners and that a purpose-built aircraft like the A-10 is a superior tank killer compared to a multirole jet like the F-16. And perhaps A-10 fans have a point. The Army's most lethal tank-killing aircraft is the AH-64 Apache attack helicopter *(pages 114-123)*. The product of a concept pioneered in the late 1960s by the United States and emulated in choppers built by the Soviet Union and France, among others, the Apache is a slow mover indeed compared to Air Force jets, with a top speed of less than 200 miles per hour. The Apache's salvation against ever more lethal air defenses lies in its ability to pick its way at low speed between woods and behind hummocks in a way that the A-10, for all its ability to hug the earth, cannot.

All such arguments, however, will remain largely academic until these weapons systems see actual combat—and the tricks an enemy pulls to defeat them. Already, reactive armor can defeat most top attack weapons. The best counter to the antitank gunship might be another helicopter armed with air-to-air missiles. Meanwhile, new weapons for both the main battle tank and its foes are moving through the design process and toward the battlefields of tomorrow.

The Future Face of Armor

As perils to tanks increase in variety, lethality, and the ability to attack the soft spots of these formidable weapons, the specter of terminal obsolescence may arise to threaten armor once again, as it did following the sobering tank losses early in the Yom Kippur War. Designers of these vehicles can postpone this day in two ways. One is to improve existing tanks. However, options on this route are eventually exhausted, as old designs prove impractical to revise for new technologies. Just as the M1 represented a complete departure from the M60, sooner or later the Abrams and its peers will demand fresh thinking and new designs.

Some improvements can be rather simply grafted onto a tank. The diverse layers of materials that constitute Chobham armor, for example, can be built as modules and attached to the tank's outer armor. When a better armor formula is devised, the modules can be replaced without having to rebuild the entire tank. Adding reactive armor—the explosive boxes that thwart shaped-charge warheads—requires little more than welding on studs to which the plaques can be bolted.

Deeper within a tank lie other technologies that can be modernized or improved without requiring a new vehicle. Engines and transmissions—the tank's power pack—are good candidates for upgrading. All that is necessary is to fit the new one into the space vacated by the old. Doing so has been difficult in the past, since more power has, with the notable exception of the turbine engine, usually resulted in a machine of larger dimensions. Ceramics research, however, promises that engineers may soon be able to mold these materials into engine parts. One advantage lies in their heat resistance. At temperatures where engines run most efficiently— well above 3,000 degrees Fahrenheit—parts made of most metals would soften or melt, even with cooling systems. Ceramics can withstand such temperatures easily and could be used to enhance both diesel and gas turbine power plants. For example, equal power could be had from a smaller engine that guzzles less fuel. Alternatively, a more powerful engine could be fit into the same space with no penalty in weight or fuel consumption.

Fire-control systems can also be refined without redesigning the entire tank or even the turret. In most M1s, the commander and gunner share a single sight, and the fire-control system can deal with only one target at a time. Only after the first of, say, two or three tanks has been hit can the gunner begin to attack the next. However, the third version of the Abrams, the M1A2, has in effect two gunsights, one for the gunner and a separate one for the tank commander. The fire-control computer and its software have been revised to permit both sights to track different targets simultaneously, a considerable advantage to a crew confronted by multiple enemies. With the new system, the commander can track a second enemy tank while the gunner deals with the first. In accepting target data from both gunsights at the same time, the computer can prepare a firing solution for two targets at once. After the gunner scores a hit, he releases the fire-control computer, which automatically lays the gun on the commander's target while the gunner begins tracking the next one.

Sensors capable of detecting various kinds of radiation are simple to add to a tank and could help defend it more quickly than the crew can react. For example, the MILES system used to score kills at the National Training Center at Fort Irwin, California, responds to the laser beams "fired" by tanks instead of live ammunition *(page 152)*. Instead of triggering a flashing yellow light to signify a hit, however, such technology might easily be adapted to automatically launch a smoke screen upon detecting a pulse from a laser range finder. Future antitank munitions may search out their targets with ultrashortwave radar signals, which are expected to provide images sufficiently clear for the weapon to distinguish between a tank and some other vehicle. A receiver on a tank could trigger a torrent of confusing signals from an on-board radar jammer. In either case, even a simple warning could alert the driver to begin vigorous evasive action to spoil the foe's firing solution. For the more distant future, experts in tank defense envision taking a step beyond reactive armor to active armor. Instead of waiting for a strike to respond, active armor systems would detect the approach of a projectile by radar and destroy it with a salvo of small projectiles fired from shotgunlike launchers embedded in the armor.

Giving a tank greater offensive firepower might seem to require little in the way of modification. In fact, however, strict limits apply to the size of a gun that will fit into a given turret. For example, a bigger gun requires heavier machinery of larger dimensions to move it. Another important constraint is recoil. Generally speaking, the bigger the bang, the heavier the recoil mechanism must be to absorb the shock. A significantly bigger gun could easily require enlarging the turret to accommodate a larger recoil system. More powerful main armament also argues for an autoloader. Even the fifty-five-pound rounds for the M1's 120-mm cannon tax the loader's ability to feed the gun as quickly as it can be aimed. Heavier cartridges would only aggravate the problem.

One future solution might be to adopt a different kind of gun altogether. Scientists at the Los Alamos National Laboratory, for example, have developed a prototype of an electromagnetic gun that uses magnetic fields to accelerate a projectile to approximately nine times the velocity of the rod penetrators fired by present guns. The experimental weapon produces very little recoil. The larger slugs needed to kill a tank could be less massive than present munitions and would require no propellant charge, an additional space-saving

advantage. However, the electrical pulse required—perhaps 600 billion watts delivered in $^2/_{1,000}$ of a second—implies generating and storage capacity that today is a long way from fitting into a tank.

Laser weapons are also a possibility, albeit a remote one pending significant progress in the technology. They also require prodigious amounts of electricity and might well prove effective only against a tank's various viewers and sensors. To penetrate a tank's armor, even a very powerful laser would have to illuminate a single spot on the target for about fifteen seconds, an eternity in battle.

Accommodating the generating capacity for such futuristic weapons—or installing a bigger turret or an autoloader to handle a larger conventional gun—demands rethinking the entire tank. For the designer, the challenge is a formidable one: to minimize the vehicle's weight while providing greater firepower and the greater protection for the crew demanded by the lethality of the modern battlefield. And all this must be accomplished as economically as possible lest the cost of an MBT escalate toward the heights occupied by the prices of modern jet fighters and bombers.

One stratagem is to reduce the so-called armored volume of the tank—that is, the space inside the tank that must be protected by its armor. The Swedish S-tank accomplishes that goal by replacing the human loader with a mechanical one. The breech of the gun is installed behind the remaining three crew members. This location permits them to sit close together, protected in part by armor and in part by the tank's machinery—engine, transmission, cooling systems, and the like. The absence of a turret on the S-tank saves additional weight; the turret of an M1, for example, weighs approximately twenty tons.

Moving the gun entirely outside the tank would also save most of the weight of a manned turret while allowing the gun to swing

Tomorrow's Threat to Armor

Raining death from the sky, the sense-and-destroy-armor (SADARM) system is the U.S. Army's first "smart" antiarmor weapon, one that can find and hit targets on its own. It attacks armored vehicles from above, where armor is relatively thin, as shown in the photographs above: A shell carrying several individual weapons, or submunitions, is fired from a cannon *(left)*. Down range, a propellant charge ejects the submunitions *(second from left)*. In the third picture, a braking parachute slows each submunition and falls away. Each submunition then deploys other parachutes that let it spin rapidly while its built-in temperature and microwave sensors scan for armored vehicles. Target acquired, the submunition detonates *(fourth picture)* and sends an explosively formed penetrator (EFP) rocketing down to smash into the target.

The diagram at right shows how the EFP is created: A disk made of a heavy, dense metal called tantalum is distorted by the aerial explosion into a projectile with a ball-shaped head and stabilizing tail fins. The entire shaping sequence takes less than $^1/_{2,500}$ of a second.

toward a target without requiring that the entire tank be pointed at it. The gun, which would be served by an autoloader, might rest on the roof between shots. To swing toward a target, the entire weapon might rise on a stalk perhaps a foot tall. The tank could be entirely concealed until just before the moment of firing, and then only the gun would be exposed. Such an arrangement could also permit the gun to be aimed downward at a steeper angle than is possible with present tanks.

No plan is without problems, and the concept for a turretless MBT has its share. In a tank with a turret, for example, the commander occupies the highest point on the vehicle. With the possible exception of a radio antenna, nothing obstructs his view of the battlefield, an important safety factor. Sitting below the gun mount in a tank without a turret, he will require some kind of television system to cover blind spots, much as some buses have TV cameras instead of mirrors to show the view directly behind. An extendible gun stalk presents hurdles of greater difficulty. The gun support must be rigid enough to take the pounding of combat, reliable to a fault, and precisely engineered for accurate fire.

Tanks of the future will evolve according to the work required of them in battle and in response to the weapons that threaten their survival, and no tank designer can see beyond the horizon with certainty. But something that fulfills the basic role of the tank has been around since the chariots of the Assyrians, the war elephants of Hannibal, and the armored knights of Arthurian legend. That is not likely to change. Tank designers will continue to find successful solutions to the ever-demanding equation of mobility, survivability, and lethality. Whatever their configuration, main battle tanks will retain their primacy in land warfare as far into the twenty-first century as military planners can see. ✮

The Tank-Busting Apache

"Send a tank to kill a tank," goes a venerable axiom of armored warfare, but new and lethal species of attack helicopters offer a fresh option.

By consensus, the deadliest of all these tank-busting choppers is the U.S. Army's AH-64A Apache. Intended to counter masses of main battle tanks, the Apache is at once swift, agile, and tough. Its twin turbine engines generate 1,800 horsepower each—enough to enable the 16,800-pound Apache to cruise at nearly 160 knots. The helicopter can withstand 3.5 Gs—three and a half times the force of gravity—in a turn, a greater stress than any other attack helicopter can tolerate. For protection, lightweight boron-carbide armor, impervious to 12.7-mm armor-piercing incendiary rounds, shields the two-man crew compartment. Some vital components are also armored, while others are positioned to minimize vulnerability. The engines, for example, are mounted six feet apart to

prevent hostile fire from damaging both.

Much is expected of these helicopters as they prowl the battlefield or range 100 miles behind enemy lines to devastate armor and other targets. Where terrain offers concealment, tacticians foresee that Apaches could kill between thirty and fifty tanks for each loss of their own.

A terrain-hugging hunter. Rolling into a steep right bank at low level, an Apache follows its leader to the target. The cylindrical pod marked No Step to the left of its Hellfire missiles holds nineteen high-velocity rockets.

Finding the Enemy around the Clock in All Weather

In the Apache, the gunner sits in the front seat, the pilot behind him. Though each can perform the other's role, the gunner's main duty is to kill tanks while the pilot flies the aircraft and takes on lesser targets with an automatic cannon mounted under the nose.

Two computer-linked optical systems—the pilot night-vision sensor (PNVS) and the target acquisition and designation sight (TADS)—allow the crew to work not only in daylight but at night, in fog or rain, and in other conditions that have always concealed and protected the enemy.

The PNVS is located in a nose turret that points in the same direction as the pilot's head. As the pilot surveys the battlefield, an infrared sensor in the PNVS detects minute variations in temperature and turns them into images projected onto video screens or onto tiny displays attached to the crew's helmets *(page 118)*. Ridges, tree lines, buildings, and other features show up clearly, enabling the crew to fly nap-of-the-earth in darkness, even when the weather is foul.

The targeting system sits in a separate nose turret. Employed primarily by the gunner, TADS has four kinds of eyes. A dual-magnification telescope—four power and eighteen power—is useful in daylight at ranges up to about 5,000 yards and is the only part of TADS to offer a view in color. Magnification up to 126 power is offered by the TADS television camera. For night operations or finding targets hidden in trees, in shadows, or behind camouflage, there is an infrared detector similar to the one in the PNVS. The fourth sensor, a laser receiver, finds and tracks targets illuminated by a pulsating laser beam from another Apache, a scout helicopter, or a team on the ground.

Loaded for action. The Apache offers its two-man crew a wide choice of weapons. Each of the four pylons beneath its wing stubs can carry four laser-guided Hellfire antitank missiles or a launch pack containing nineteen folding-fin unguided rockets for use against softer targets such as enemy troops and vehicles. Depending on the mission, a full load could be either sixteen Hellfires, seventy-six of the folding-fin, spin-stabilized rockets, or a combination of both. The 30-mm chain-gun automatic cannon is named for the electrically powered chain drive that, instead of propellant gases or recoil from each shot, operates the weapon. Extremely resistant to jamming from misfires, the mechanism draws ammunition from a 1,200-round magazine at the rate of ten rounds per second. The cannon's high-explosive, armor-piercing bullets can destroy armored personnel carriers, vehicles, and other aircraft. They are lethal against troops out to 4,000 yards.

MULTIPURPOSE ROCKETS

HELLFIRE MISSILES

CHAIN GUN

TADS

PNVS

INFRARED SENSOR

INFRARED SENSOR

LASER TRACKER

TELEVISION

TELESCOPE

LASER DESIGNATOR

Eagle eyes. **A closeup view shows details of the PNVS and TADS installations in the Apache's nose. Independently swiveling turrets allow the PNVS to look upward as much as twenty degrees, down forty-five degrees, and ninety degrees left or right. The TADS has even greater coverage—thirty degrees up, sixty degrees down, and 120 degrees left or right—permitting the gunner to lock onto a target that he can see only by looking over his shoulder.**

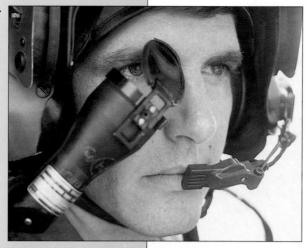

An electronic eyepiece. This helmet-mounted device displays infrared images from the PNVS. Though the one-inch monocle seems too close to focus on, the system projects the image so that the eye feels as if it is looking at something far away. The monocle also displays target information and, when linked to the PNVS, data needed to fly the aircraft without glancing at the instrument panel.

PROJECTOR   SENSORS

Tracking the head. A pair of sensors and an infrared projector enable the Apache's turrets and chain gun to follow the gaze of pilot or gunner. Each of the crew first holds his head to center his monocle cross hairs on the helicopter's boresight reticle, then presses a button to establish a head-orientation baseline. In operation, the projector sweeps two beams down the side of the helmet twenty-five times a second. Each sensor emits a distinctive signal at a different time depending on headgear angle, providing sufficient data for a computer to calculate where a crew member is looking.

The gunner's view. The green display glowing in front of the gunner can show either television or infrared TADS scenes. To see through the telescope, the gunner leans forward to the circular eyepiece above the screen. The circular lens atop the instrument panel is called a boresight reticle; it is a vital part of the system that allows the crew to electronically align their monocles with the PNVS, TADS, and weapons before takeoff.

Flying and Fighting Aids for the Crew

On a combat mission, an Apache pilot typically flies "head up," peering outside the aircraft and aided under adverse conditions by a helmet monocle that superimposes flight, weapons, and navigation information on a PNVS infrared image. The system points both the PNVS and the chain gun wherever the pilot looks.

The pilot can also pass a target to the TADS, operated by the gunner, for attack by rocket or Hellfire missile. To do so, the pilot gunner simply turns to position his monocle cross hairs on the quarry, and the gunner flips a switch that points the TADS at the target. When using the TADS himself, the gunner points the turret at a target by means of a control under his right thumb. With the cross hairs on the target, pressing a button tells the TADS to lock on.

Next, the Apache's primary computer takes over, continually recalculating firing solutions whenever the helicopter changes altitude, speed, or direction, or when the target moves. Says an Apache pilot: "Once it's locked in, it won't get away."

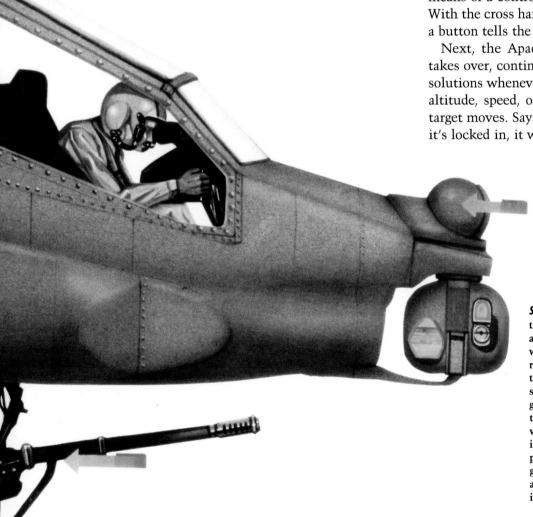

Separate masters. Red arrows in the illustration of the Apache attack helicopter at left show which aircraft systems typically respond to the pilot, who controls the PNVS and chain gun simply by turning his head. The gunner, who normally directs the TADS assembly, does so with hand controls. The TADS is precisely stabilized to provide a steady view of a target even at great magnifications and during vigorous maneuvering by the pilot.

A Deadly Weapon for Every Target

Which weapon the Apache uses in combat depends on the target under attack. Both the 70-mm rockets and the 30-mm chain gun are regarded as area weapons. Besides being used against lightly armored vehicles such as personnel carriers, they are typically fired at troop concentrations, aircraft parked on the ground, ammunition-storage areas, and antiaircraft defenses. The rockets have twice the range of and are more flexible than the gun. In addition to high-explosive warheads, they can deliver infantry-crippling antipersonnel mines, grenades, aircraft-shredding fléchettes, and other munitions. Furthermore, they can be fired singly or in pairs, quads, or a salvo of up to seventy-six rockets. The rocket launcher can tilt four degrees up or fifteen degrees down to adjust for target distance as determined by the laser designator employed as a range finder. However, the launcher does not swing from side to side as the gun does, making it necessary for the pilot or gunner to turn the entire helicopter toward the target before firing.

To kill tanks, an Apache will launch its primary weapon—the AGM-114 Hellfire missile. Steered by a sophisticated laser-guidance system, the hundred-pound Hellfire packs a seventeen-pound shaped charge *(pages 72-75)* that can penetrate the armor of all known main battle tanks. As shown at far right and on the following pages, there is a broad range of tactics—some requiring advance coordination between participants—for employing these versatile missiles.

A joint assault. Though the Apache can illuminate a target for a Hellfire missile with its own laser beam, security lies in having someone else do the job. In the illustration at right, a Kiowa scout helicopter, exposing only a sphere atop the rotor that contains a laser designator, illuminates a distant tank for an Apache using a ridge for concealment. The gunner launches a Hellfire missile in the general direction of the target. As the Hellfire streaks above the ridge, the field of view of a laser seeker in the missile's nose takes in the laser-lit tank *(left)* and steers the weapon toward it.

Using multiple designators. Masked by a ridge, an AH-64 launches a pair of missiles in the direction of tanks illuminated by two remote laser designators—one aimed by an infantryman, the other trained from a Kiowa scout helicopter. Before launch, the designators are programmed to emit—and the Hellfire seekers to sense—laser pulses in different patterns or pulse codes. Fired no more than a second or two apart, the missiles climb above the high ground, then zero in on the laser spots they were tuned to detect. Every eight seconds, the Apache gunner launches another pair of Hellfires, which are well on their way when the previous pair strikes. The designators quickly aim at new targets for the follow-on missiles. Proceeding in this manner, a single Apache can fire a full load of sixteen Hellfire missiles, each at a different target, in less than a minute—fast enough to destroy an entire tank company before it has time to react.

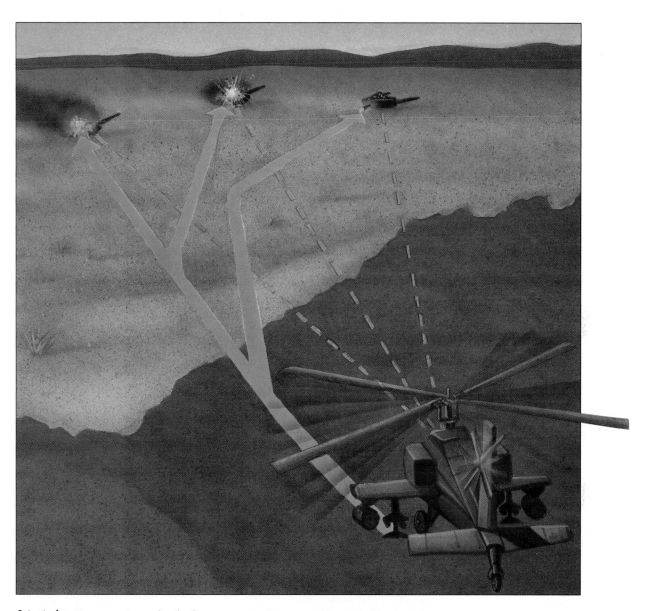

Going it alone. Encountering a clutch of tanks but lacking the time to coordinate with operators of other laser designators, an Apache can still mount a devastating assault with the rapid-fire option shown above. Rising suddenly from behind a sheltering crag, the AH-64 launches three Hellfire missiles at intervals of seven to ten seconds. Initially, all three home on the first target illuminated by the helicopter's on-board laser designator. When the first missile strikes its target, the gunner quickly swings the laser to the next tank, causing the remaining missiles to change course. Then, when the second Hellfire strikes home, the gunner re-aims the designator to light up the third tank for the final Hellfire.

To the Ends of the Earth

Painted desert tan, M1 Abrams tanks of the 24th Division jam the dock at Savannah, Georgia, ready for shipment to Saudi Arabia aboard one of the Navy's eight fast sealift ships. In the foreground, a soldier secures a roll of barbed wire to the rear deck of an M1.

Watching their M1 Abrams tanks roll onto railroad flatcars and out of Fort Stewart, Georgia, on August 10, 1990, the men of Company B could not help feeling uneasy. The big tanks were beginning a 12,000-mile journey to Saudi Arabia, scene of a rapid military buildup to deter any further advance by the Iraqi forces that had just overrun the little nation of Kuwait. Company B's tankers, like other troops of the 24th Infantry Division (Mechanized), would be reunited with their equipment at a Persian Gulf port by the end of the month. But with the prospect of combat suddenly so real, they found it hard to be without their familiar fighting machines for even a brief time, unable to practice the movements they might use in battle. So Company B ("Buzzards," they had begun calling themselves, after the sharp-eyed scavengers that circle in the desert skies) availed themselves of an alternative: Lacking their M1s, they would practice in golf carts.

Fourteen of the humble vehicles were borrowed from the pro at the Fort Stewart golf course. The Buzzard tank commanders and drivers donned their chemical-warfare attire—hooded gas masks and loose-fitting suits made to repel liquids and filter out chemicals and germs. They then proceeded onto the fairways and re-created the tank formations learned on the training field, jouncing over the lush landscape in an unlikely simulation of maneuver and attack.

For the drivers, who have little peripheral vision in an Abrams and no vision at all to the rear, the 360-degree view of the golf-cart session proved particularly enlightening. Said one: "It gave me a chance to see what the battlefield looked like and how important my role is to the entire team."

The Buzzards' fairway practice was one of the few activities of the 24th Infantry Division not spelled out in a tight script written long beforehand. Together with Marines and airborne troops numbering in the tens of thousands, the 24th was part of a swift and massive deployment of ground forces that would have been impossible without detailed preparation and planning. In the space of just three weeks, the entire division, 16,600 strong, would race almost halfway around the world, perhaps to fight against a well-trained and well-equipped enemy in a land having one of the harshest environments on earth.

Merely conveying the troops to the scene was, by itself, an enormous challenge—but it paled in comparison to the task of transporting the divisional matériel. Among the 24th Infantry's vehicles and weapons were 200 M1 Abrams tanks, 400 M2 Bradley fighting vehicles mounting rapid-firing Bushmaster 25-mm automatic cannons, 50 M198 self-propelled 155-mm artillery pieces, 8 tracked, multiple-launch rocket systems (MLRS), and 300 HMMWV multipurpose vehicles (humvees). Lighter gear included 28,560 MOPP chemical protection suits, 16,600 M17 protective masks, and 128 truckloads of ammunition. Among the expendables were 15 tons of medical supplies, 1.5 million ready-to-eat meals, 33 tons of hamburger meat, 85 tons of fruit and vegetables, 25,000 gallons of bottled water, 42,500 water-purification tablets, 25,500 bottles of sunscreen, 1,020 boxes of lip balm, 39,000 containers of foot powder, 20,000 pairs of sunglasses, and 3,000 handkerchiefs.

Only a few years before, a deployment on this scale and at this speed would have been inconceivable—and even now it was an enterprise of staggering complexity. It required special planes, special ships, and all manner of supporting gear, from the towering gantry crane that rolls shoreside on railroad tracks for loading the ships to a computer system called LOGMARS, which catalogs the dimensions and weight of each item on the manifest and calculates an optimum loading plan. Above all, forethought and foresight made it possible for America to thrust a daunting mass of armor in front of Saddam Hussein's 100,000-man force even before the in-

Sea routes from two widely separated embarkation points converged in the Gulf of Oman leading into the Persian Gulf. These were the routes taken by ships steaming to Saudi Arabia laden with heavy equipment for Operation Desert Shield. The fast sealift ships, which had departed from the U.S. East Coast, crossed the Atlantic and sailed through the Mediterranean (upper left). Then they entered the Red Sea via the Suez Canal, and rounded the tip of the Arabian Peninsula by way of the Gulf of Aden and the Arabian Sea. The 12,000-mile voyage took ten to fourteen days, depending on the weight of the cargo.

By contrast, the ships of the Maritime Prepositioning Force, stationed at Diego Garcia in the Indian Ocean's Chagos Archipelago, made the 2,500-mile journey in five to seven days.

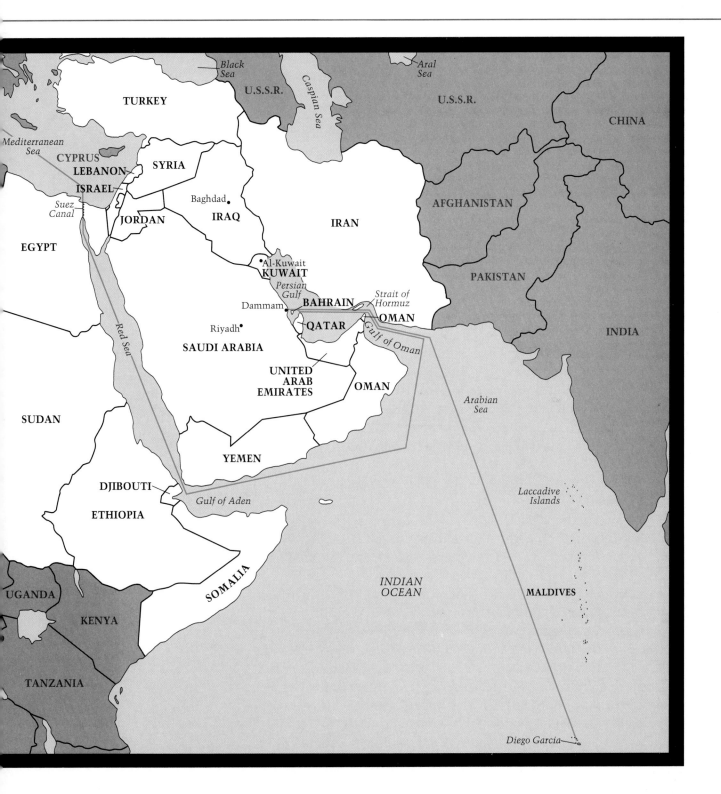

vaders had time to digest their first rich morsel and perhaps prepare for the next course.

The story begins in 1979, when a group of military planners started to consider how the United States could quickly react to a future threat outside Europe. They chose a scenario that could hardly have been more apt: They imagined the very event that would send the 24th Division eastward—an invasion of Kuwait by Iraq.

A Master Plan for Distant Contingencies

On a blazing-hot summer's day in 1979, Air Force General David C. Jones, chairman of the United States Joint Chiefs of Staff, received a call summoning him from his Pentagon office to the White House. No sooner had he arrived than he found himself subjected to an unexpected grilling by aides of President Jimmy Carter. The general was asked about progress in fulfilling the mandate of Presidential Directive 18, an August 1977 decision to create a rapid deployment force of 100,000 that could be dispatched to the Middle East, Southeast Asia, or some other distant hot spot should American interests there become seriously threatened. President Carter was particularly concerned about potential political destabilization in the oil-producing lands surrounding the Persian Gulf.

It was an uncomfortable session. The nation's top military officer had to admit that not much had been done. Jones returned to the Pentagon and called in Army Major General Charles Dyke, vice-director of operations on Jones's staff. He told Dyke to handpick an action cell of fifteen colleagues and go to work on the problem. Dyke promptly assembled a team, drawing most of its members from among the planners working for the Joint Chiefs of Staff. The fifteen represented the Defense Intelligence Agency, the Air Force, the Marines, special- and joint-operations forces, the Army Signal Corps, and the Defense Nuclear Agency. Missing from the lineup was the Navy, which provided experts on an ad hoc basis whenever naval matters were considered. The team chief was Air Force Colonel Thomas Thaanum, an expert on moving things by air.

General Charles Dyke headed the 1979 Contingency Review Group (CRG), which produced a study that set in motion a decade-long expansion of the U.S. military's capability for rapid deployment abroad. A much-decorated former company commander in Korea and battalion commander in Vietnam, Dyke worked in the late 1970s for the Joint Chiefs of Staff, as did most of the fifteen planners he chose for the CRG.

Dubbed the Contingency Review Group (CRG), they were allotted a small suite of offices just across the corridor from the National Military Command Center, which collects and continually updates information on the status of America's armed forces and those of potential opponents. Jones personally gave the planners their marching orders. He instructed the CRG to consider an American military and naval movement to the Persian Gulf; it was to be a major operation but not a superpower confrontation. The planners were to identify the problems posed by such a deployment, recommend solutions, and get the job done within sixty days.

There were good reasons for Dyke's team to choose a hypothetical invasion of Kuwait as a scenario: The Iraqis had long asserted that the tiny emirate was rightfully theirs; once it was considered a part of Basra—now a province of Iraq. But it had been semi-autonomous even under Ottoman Turkish rule (1288-1918) and was a self-governing British protectorate from 1918 until it gained independence in 1961. Shortly thereafter, Iraq had threatened to reclaim its alleged territory and punctuated its aggressive words with minor Iraqi border crossings. This conduct triggered a British reaction. To protect Kuwait, the United Kingdom deployed troops from a base at Aden and landed Royal Marines from the Mediterranean fleet.

Within two weeks of setting the objective, the Contingency Review Group had taken the measure of the task. At the time, Iraq had ten divisions, six of them armored. To counter an Iraqi offensive, the United States would need a large combined-arms force of infantry, artillery, and tanks, which typically might include two mechanized infantry divisions, two airborne divisions, and two Army Ranger battalions. Three amphibious Marine brigades would also likely be needed. And because the various units must have tactical air support, three aircraft carriers would also be required, along with an unestimated but considerable number of Air Force fighters and enough airlift to ferry supplies.

The U.S. Marines—necessary early in any deployment to help secure a foothold for the buildup of other forces—could quickly deploy to the Persian Gulf a battalion 800 strong; such a unit was almost always afloat in the Mediterranean Sea with the Sixth Fleet, about a week's steaming time from the Gulf by way of the Suez Canal, an interval that would stretch to approximately six weeks if Egypt denied the fleet passage. Fielding a full brigade of 15,000 leathernecks and their supplies would take at least a month, maybe two. But that was the good news. Moving the whole invasion-countering force into place would take eight to ten months—a decidedly unrapid deployment.

Part of the reason was the deplorable state of the nation's sealift resources. The Department of Defense had always counted on U.S. merchant shipping and the so-called mothball fleet, a reserve stock of mostly World War II-era freighters and tankers that supposedly could be renovated and made operational. Dyke's investigators soon found that the mothball fleet was a collection of elderly hulks incapable of speedy activation. It would take many months to strip off the protective coverings, repair the rusted hulls, rehabilitate the ancient power plants, and install communications equipment.

There was, however, a minifleet, comprising twenty-eight Navy ships of more recent vintage. They were known as the Ready Reserve Force and were supposedly available for service within ten days of being tapped for duty. But the Dyke team had no confidence that a call-up would work as advertised. The ships had no crews assigned to them; there was not even a pool of unassigned seamen from which crews could be drawn.

Pentagon planners explored the use of commercial carriers but discovered that the United States had become heavily dependent on foreign-owned and foreign-operated maritime transport. Low-cost overseas shipyards and minimum-wage seamen from other nations had almost driven the United States out of the shipping business. The U.S. merchant fleet had dwindled to a handful of supertankers, container ships, and other specialized types. All were fully employed, carrying cargo throughout the world. In theory, the military could commandeer them for sealift purposes. But the ships would have to steam for port, off-load their cargoes, then make their way to military embarkation points. Weeks would pass. Furthermore, some of the ships might be carrying strategically important materials. Switching cargoes could interfere with other military objectives or damage the U.S. economy.

Equally inadequate was the nation's capacity for transporting an expeditionary force by air. The CRG found there was only enough airlift, both commercial and military, to rapidly deliver and support one airborne division and a few tactical fighter squadrons. The delivery of the single, lightly armored 82d Airborne to the Persian Gulf would take twenty-six days.

In the matter of airlift, however, remedies were available. Team chief Thaanum, the air logistics expert, brought to the CRG's attention three projects that could dramatically improve the situation. They had been developed by teams of military and industrial engineers, but had mostly languished for lack of funds and congressional support.

The first project involved the existing fleet of Lockheed C-141 Starlifter jet transports, the backbone of U.S. intercontinental military airlift. When introduced in 1965, the C-141 cut in half the cost of delivering a ton of cargo by air and reduced the delivery time by one-third. Dyke's team examined the merits of "stretching" the C-141, a kind of surgical procedure that the plane's maker, Lockheed Aeronautical Systems Company, had been pushing since the early 1970s. The operation called for each fuselage to be sliced completely through at two points, fore and aft. At each cut, the segments would be pulled apart, and a "plug" inserted amounting to an extension of the body more than twenty-three feet. Stretching the jet transport would increase its capacity by 30 percent. At the same time, the planes would be fitted with plumbing for midair refueling. Eliminating refueling stops would be a major timesaver, allowing many more sorties by the C-141s.

A second project to increase air-transport proficiency focused on the world's largest cargo plane, the Lockheed C-5 Galaxy, used to carry heavy, bulky items such as helicopters and self-propelled cannons. The CRG estimated that the available C-5 airlift potential fell 28 percent short of that needed for the hypothetical Persian Gulf deployment, in part because the mammoth planes wore out too quickly. Cracks were appearing in the wings after only 7,000 flying hours, about one-quarter of the expected service life. Thaanum suggested accelerating an existing but underfunded program to "rewing" the C-5 fleet by reconstructing and strengthening the plane's frame at its wing root cap, the point in the fuselage where the wings are attached. A shortened rewinging schedule could be completed by 1988, adding years to each C-5's life and increasing its lift capacity by 25 percent to 295,000 tons.

A troubled air resupply of Israel during the 1973 Yom Kippur War weighed heavily in the thinking of Dyke's team when it looked at a third airlift enhancement project: adding to the small fleet of KC-10 Extender high-capacity aerial tankers. In 1973, the U.S. emergency replenishing of Israel's quickly diminishing ammuni-

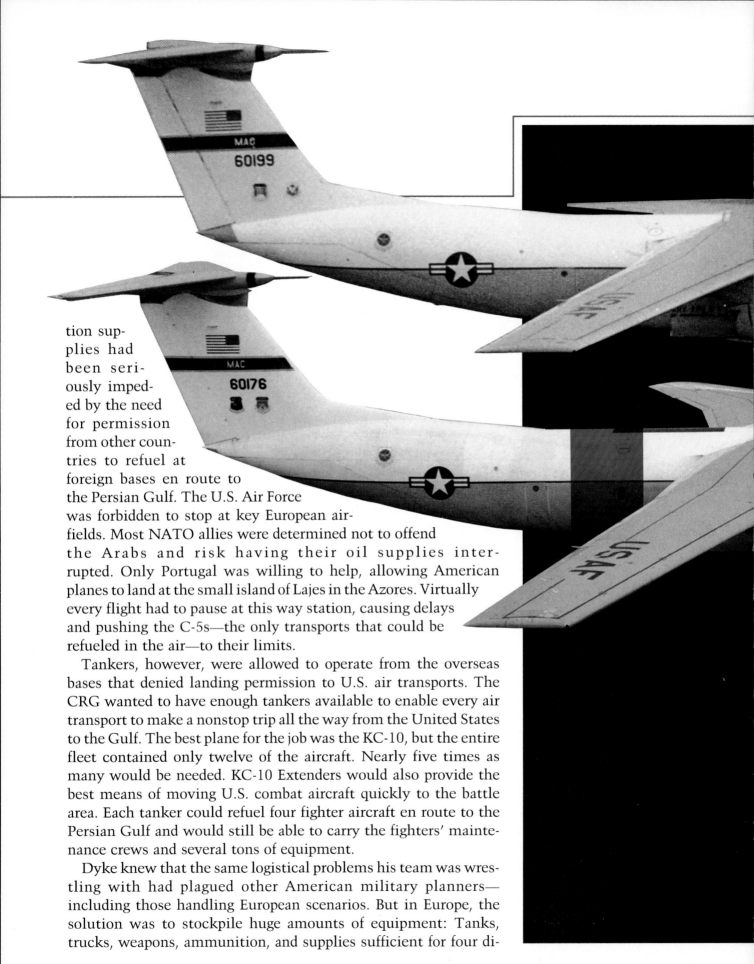

tion sup-
plies had
been seri-
ously imped-
ed by the need
for permission
from other coun-
tries to refuel at
foreign bases en route to
the Persian Gulf. The U.S. Air Force
was forbidden to stop at key European airfields. Most NATO allies were determined not to offend
the Arabs and risk having their oil supplies inter-
rupted. Only Portugal was willing to help, allowing American
planes to land at the small island of Lajes in the Azores. Virtually
every flight had to pause at this way station, causing delays
and pushing the C-5s—the only transports that could be
refueled in the air—to their limits.

Tankers, however, were allowed to operate from the overseas
bases that denied landing permission to U.S. air transports. The
CRG wanted to have enough tankers available to enable every air
transport to make a nonstop trip all the way from the United States
to the Gulf. The best plane for the job was the KC-10, but the entire
fleet contained only twelve of the aircraft. Nearly five times as
many would be needed. KC-10 Extenders would also provide the
best means of moving U.S. combat aircraft quickly to the battle
area. Each tanker could refuel four fighter aircraft en route to the
Persian Gulf and would still be able to carry the fighters' maintenance crews and several tons of equipment.

Dyke knew that the same logistical problems his team was wres-
tling with had plagued other American military planners—
including those handling European scenarios. But in Europe, the
solution was to stockpile huge amounts of equipment: Tanks,
trucks, weapons, ammunition, and supplies sufficient for four di-

visions were on hand. Troops flown there from the United States could go into action immediately.

This scheme, known as prepositioning, was not generally considered as an option for the Persian Gulf. Although some of the Arab states wanted the United States to defend them in an emergency, governments in the region would not permit U.S. bases and supply depots on their soil. They were disinclined to risk the political problems that a permanent American military presence might create. Furthermore, persuading local powers to store military equipment would only raise another problem. Without the presence of American combat units to provide security, there was no assurance that prepositioned equipment would be safe in a Persian Gulf storage site. The revolution in Iran, transforming that country from an ally to an implacable enemy overnight, was a grim reminder of what could happen.

But there was an alternative to prepositioning on land: prepositioning at sea. A maritime version of advance stockpiling might at least serve for the early-arriving forces in a rapid deployment operation. Maritime prepositioning called for stashing equipment aboard ships that would be kept within easy sailing distance of a potential trouble spot. The equipment would be stored in dehumidified compartments and cargo holds to prevent deterioration in the salt air. When the call to action came, the ships would proceed to a port close by a secure airfield in the target area. Troops would then be flown to the airfield and matched up with their equipment and supplies. Because ships can carry vastly more cargo than planes, this approach would be faster than shuttling all the hardware and stocks in by air. It would also permit the use of heavier forces.

Maritime prepositioning had worked two decades earlier, when the U.S. Army moored ships off Okinawa to store the equipment of a brigade based in Hawaii. During a threat to the kingdom of Laos by North Vietnam and Laotian rebels in 1961, a brigade from the U.S. 25th Infantry Division was flown to Thailand from Hawaii while the ships containing the unit's equipment were moved from

The fuselage of the "stretched" Lockheed C-141B Starlifter *(bottom)* is more than twenty-three feet longer than the C-141A above it. Extensions *(shaded areas)* were made both fore and aft of the wings to preserve aerodynamic balance. Because of the C-141B's added capacity, Lockheed recommended strengthening the aircraft's wings, but the Air Force demurred at the $168 million cost—and wisely so. Even though eight years later, during Operation Desert Shield, nineteen of the 266 transports were grounded for wing cracks, the cost of repairing each of them came to less than $300,000.

A mammoth C-5 Galaxy transport aircraft can swallow as many as six AH-64 Apache attack helicopters while providing seventy-five seats for flight and maintenance crews. The plane's dimensions are prodigious. Tires stand more than four feet tall. The tail juts sixty-five feet into the air. Wings stretch three-quarters the length of a football field, and the cockpit sits more than three stories above the ground.

Okinawa to a Thai port. The brigade was joined to the equipment and the force was moved to central Thailand, near the Laotian border. Although efforts to end the insurgency failed, the deployment was hailed as a success.

All in all, maritime prepositioning looked like a good bet, as did the various ideas for enhanced airlift. After two months, the CRG submitted its recommendations. They proposed anchoring a fleet of loaded transports within easy striking distance of the Persian Gulf, stretching the C-141s, rewinging the C-5s, and buying forty-four new KC-10 tankers. The CRG report also stated that if the Pentagon wanted sealift adequate for a large-scale rapid deployment, it would have to create its own fleet. But it need not build the ships from scratch. The group urged the military to buy and modify an existing fleet of eight huge, fast, commercial container ships then owned by the Sea-Land Corporation, a company that had fallen on hard times.

Taken together, these various measures would ensure the ability of the United States to move a sizable force to the Persian Gulf in a hurry. Still, the recommendations were undeniably complex and expensive. Many of them had been proposed before in one form or another but had been ignored or given only token funding. To veteran staff officers, the CRG's "think big" study was one more in a long line of futile Pentagon paper drills. None of the CRG's officers believed their proposals would ever be fully realized.

Building on a Prescient Blueprint

On January 23, 1980, President Carter, responding to the Soviet Union's invasion of Afghanistan the previous December, declared the Persian Gulf to be a region of vital U.S. interest. In the wake of this policy statement (soon known as the Carter Doctrine), priorities began shifting in the Department of Defense. Particularly affected were the Contingency Review Group's lineal heirs, a team of military planners called the Rapid Deployment Joint Task Force (RDJTF), which had been established by Secretary of Defense Harold Brown a month earlier and was composed largely of CRG staffers. At the time, their prospects for funds and attention had seemed dim. Now the RDJTF was hot.

Secretary Brown had named Marine Lieutenant General Paul X. Kelley to command the task force, headquartered at MacDill Air

Force Base in Florida. He had some highly suitable experience. Back in 1961, when the British entered Kuwait to deter an Iraqi invasion, Kelley had been on the scene as an exchange officer.

Charged with moving those blueprints toward actuality, Kelley and the RDJTF staff set about finding a safe and secure anchorage for transport ships to be prepositioned near the Persian Gulf. Diego Garcia seemed to fill the bill. This muggy and isolated chip of British territory in the middle of the Indian Ocean lay five to seven days' sailing time (less than 2,500 miles) from the Persian Gulf. The island, thirteen square miles in area, was a Royal Navy outpost and doubled as a U.S. Navy refueling and communications way station under a casual arrangement with the United Kingdom.

Washington proposed to greatly expand Diego Garcia's sparse facilities, and the British agreed (despite a protest from local officials, who saw their placid lifestyle coming to an end). More than $200 million in American building funds were poured into construction work over the next few years. The existing airfield was a small strip known among the aviation community for an unusual landing hazard—a herd of obstinate and free-wandering donkeys. The airfield was vastly improved, fenced, and lengthened. The harbor was dredged and a 2,000-foot wharf was built. Fuel and water storage was increased, and maintenance facilities, a mess and sleeping quarters, hangars, and storage sites were added.

By 1986, the work was mostly finished, and five large, fully loaded transports were lying at anchor in the harbor. Under the care of a skeleton staff, they were ready to receive crews for a rapid transit to the Gulf. Although some of the floating matériel at Diego Garcia was Army and Air Force munitions and stocks, the bulk belonged to the Marine Corps. The five-ship Diego Garcia Maritime Prepositioning Squadron (MPS) contained enough equipment and supplies for a 15,000-troop Marine brigade—including its air-support element—to fight for thirty days.

Within a single MPS ship were as many as 1,400 vehicles, all sealed in air-conditioned compartments that wrung the humidity from the sea air. The ship carried its own ramps for unloading vehicles, had a large helicopter landing pad on the deck, and even stored some small cargo-handling landing craft for off-loading operations in situations where there was no dock. In the ship was stored as much as 230,000 cubic feet of ammunition and another 100,000 cubic feet of general supplies. Mammoth liquid storage containers held 540,000 gallons of diesel fuel, 855,000 gallons of aviation fuel, 200,000 gallons of gasoline, and 82,000 gallons of drinking water. The water supply could be linked to a special delivery system—a pump and hose apparatus that could be stretched two miles inland to reach thirsty Marines. One of the MPS ships contained a 280-bed hospital, complete with operating rooms.

Plans called for this floating supply and support base to be maintained under a commercial contract between an American company and the Navy. The ships were to be emptied every two years so that equipment could be exchanged, rotated, or modified if necessary. On an alert, the commercial company was obligated to provide full crews; they would sail under Navy control and with Navy combatant escorts.

Maritime prepositioning was, of course, only one piece of the rapid-deployment puzzle. Kelley and his successors at the RDJTF—newly renamed Central Command (CENTCOM)—constantly pressed for all the airlift programs that the CRG had advocated. And they got their way. By early 1990, the overall airlift-improvement endeavor—the stretched C-141s, the rewinged C-5As, and the additional KC-10 Extenders—was complete. In the space of ten years, the Military Airlift Command's transport capacity had been increased by almost 90 percent.

But neither maritime prepositioning nor airlift enhancement could move armor to the Persian Gulf in sizable amounts. The Marine Brigade prepositioning package contained fifty-three M60 main battle tanks. Additionally, the 82d Airborne Division, a unit that could arrive even sooner than the Marines, had about fifty air-transportable M551 Sheridan light tanks, each weighing seventeen tons. But these Marine and Army tank units were not organized, equipped, or trained for the wide-ranging slugfests and rapid sweeps that characterize modern armored warfare. The Marines use armor to support riflemen. The 82d Airborne's missile-firing Sheridans were suitable only in a defensive, antitank role. Both the Marines and the paratroopers keyed the pace of their few tanks to the foot soldier. So Kelley turned to the CRG's other sealift option—the purchase of a fleet of commercial container ships from the New Jersey-based Sea-Land Corporation.

The ships were for sale at a deep discount. In the early 1970s—heady days of low-cost oil and a booming world economy—Sea-Land had gambled and lost. The company had ordered eight

Some of the ships needed to store the supplies and equipment of a U.S. Marine amphibious brigade lie anchored off Diego Garcia in the Indian Ocean in 1983. At right, sitting low in the water, are two heavily laden tankers. The large ships at center and left are dry cargo vessels. In the foreground is part of a lagoon that laps against the thirteen-square-mile horseshoe-shaped coral atoll.

ships built at Dutch and German shipyards, thinking to capture a high percentage of the new container-shipping trade by creating big, specially fitted vessels that were easy to load and unload. To further sharpen their competitive edge, the container ships would be fast— capable of making thirty-three knots (thirty-eight miles per hour), as compared to the average freighter's twenty knots. Called SL-7s (Sea-Land model 7), the ships achieved that speed with a pair of massive steam-turbine engines that developed a total of 120,000 horsepower. Two boilers generated the steam for the turbines by burning fuel oil—huge amounts of it.

That was the problem. After the Arab-Israeli Yom Kippur War in 1973, oil prices rose steeply. The fuel required to propel one of the ships at a somewhat relaxed speed of twenty-six knots cost at least $70,000 per day. By 1979, the Sea-Land Corporation could no longer afford to operate its proud new fleet. Although the SL-7s had cost $53 million each, the company was willing to sell them for only about $32 million apiece.

Military logisticians were attracted to the SL-7s as much for their carrying capacity as for their speed. Each SL-7 was 946 feet long, more than the length of three football fields and almost the size of a modern nuclear aircraft carrier. Together, the eight ships would be able to transport 9,000 vehicles as well as 143,360 tons of equipment and supplies. And once they were loaded, the vessels could convey the matériel of an entire armored division from the United States to Europe in five days or to the Persian Gulf in two weeks. Subsequently, the SL-7s could swiftly return to the United States and pick up the equipment and supplies of another armored or mechanized division.

There was, however, a catch. The SL-7s were designed to be loaded and unloaded entirely by hoist. But the logistics officers who favored buying the SL-7 fleet wanted a quicker system. They recommended reconfiguring the SL-7 fleet into a so-called roll on/roll off (RO/RO) design. Giant doors would be built into the hulls, and ramps would be constructed internally to connect the six decks of each ship. Much of the cargo would consist of layer on layer of tanks and other vehicles that could simply be driven on, lashed down, then driven off at the destination.

The Department of Defense backed Kelley's team and convinced Congress that buying the SL-7s was economical as well as efficient and tactically sound. Moving an American armored or mechanized division to the Persian Gulf by the C-5 and C-141 air fleets would require 2,100 sorties and would cost $1.65 per pound. The SL-7 fleet could perform the job for about a dime per pound.

In addition to the purchase funds, Congress authorized an additional $375 million to pay for the conversion of the ships to RO/RO design. The first converted SL-7 was turned over to the Navy in 1984, and by 1986 all eight were classed as United States Navy Ships (USNS), a designation indicating civilian-crewed vessels belonging to the U.S. Navy. Instead of SL-7s, they became known as fast sealift ships (FSS). Four were kept at ports in the Gulf of Mexico, the others along the East Coast.

Since the fast sealift ships would put to sea only in an emergency or during an exercise, a commercial contract much like the one used for the MPS fleet was arranged. The FSS were maintained by nine-man civilian skeleton crews; the commercial contractor had to be capable of bringing each vessel up to its full complement of thirty-three within ninety-six hours.

While working to turn the major recommendations of the CRG into a reality, CENTCOM ventured into an area that Dyke's team had rejected; it revived the idea of prepositioning armored equipment in the Persian Gulf region—specifically, in Saudi Arabia. That country had a long association with the U.S. Army. In the early 1980s, the Corps of Engineers was in its fifteenth year of a $14 billion Saudi-funded construction program to create a modern communications and transportation infrastructure, which included

An Israeli Offer: Armor Wrapped to Go

In 1981, when the U.S. Rapid Deployment Joint Task Force was seeking a prepositioning partner among the Arab countries, Israeli Defense Minister Ariel Sharon offered U.S. Secretary of Defense Caspar Weinberger an array of hardware already in place in the Middle East. The proposal might have solved the dilemma America faced—meeting the need for instant military readiness in the Persian Gulf region.

At locations throughout the barren Negev Desert, the Israeli Army had the equipment of several armored divisions and other units in storage, maintained and guarded by a skeleton crew. If there was an alert, hundreds of school buses could quickly follow well-rehearsed routes to pick up members of reserve army units in populated areas. These citizen-warriors would then be driven to the desert storage sites.

Even in a region as dry as the Negev, there is occasionally enough moisture to cause corrosion. And during periods of extremely low humidity, vital gun and brake seals can dry out. The stored Israeli equipment, therefore, was not exposed to the elements but was kept in a carefully controlled and sealed environment. Each vehicle was sealed in a specially tailored protection bag. This large plastic cocoon, which was equipped with a humidity-control system and a battery charger to keep the vehicle's batteries topped off, kept a tank, for exam-

ple, ready for combat at a moment's notice.

At the Sharon-Weinberger meeting in 1981, Israel offered to make available from its own stocks in the Negev Desert an entire division's roster of armor—M60 tanks, M113 armored personnel carriers, and 155-mm tracked and armored artillery pieces. The equipment was to be stored and maintained by the Israeli Army for use by the U.S. Rapid Deployment Force. If the Americans added wheeled tank transporters to the mix, they could quickly dispatch an armored division to almost any hot spot in the Middle East.

Despite the obvious advantages of this plan, it had little chance of acceptance. The dispute between Israel and its Arab neighbors was so deep-rooted that if a secret American storage site in Israel was discovered—as it surely would be—U.S. credibility in the Arab states would plummet. It was also unlikely that any Arab state would permit transit of an American armored force coming out of Israel.

The issue was still being discussed in 1982, when Israel invaded Lebanon. Relations between Israel and the United States cooled, and most deals with the Israelis then under consideration were dropped.

well-furnished naval and air bases. Adding on a few facilities seemed an easy thing to do.

The corps was scheduled to have its busiest construction year in Saudi Arabia in 1983, with $1.78 billion worth of projects at hundreds of construction sites, the employment of 3,000 American supervisors, and the labor of several hundred thousand workers. In a huge land with so much construction in progress, a few scattered and discreet storage sites might not attract much attention.

At the urging of CENTCOM, the State Department pressed for assurances that the bases being built by the Corps of Engineers in Saudi Arabia could be used by Americans in the event of an emergency. But the Saudis continued to reject U.S. appeals. In 1985, an agreement outlining U.S. technical help was signed, but it was laced with restrictive conditions that made prepositioning impossible. The most the United States could achieve was an indication from

Rehearsals in Egypt

Tanks and troops advance across the Egyptian sands during Operation Bright Star in 1990. In the two-day war games, U.S. forces practiced navigating by compass and judging distances on a terrain all but devoid of landmarks that soldiers usually count on as reference points. Meanwhile, U.S. officers worked with their Egyptian counterparts on ways to integrate operations.

the Saudis that the bases would be "overbuilt," providing more space and more facilities than the Saudis themselves needed. This modest extra margin could be used by forces sent to assist the kingdom in a crisis. But nothing more than occasional and temporary guest status was contemplated. Permanent prepositioning of a significant amount of armor was simply not in the cards.

A Masterful Realization

The order sending the 24th Infantry Division (Mechanized) to Saudi Arabia originated in the office of the Joint Chiefs of Staff on August 8, 1990, where it was fed into an encryption machine to become a jumble of random-seeming letters. When the message clattered out of a decryption machine at Fort Stewart, Georgia, the communica-

The Saudi Arabian climate and terrain held few surprises for Desert Shield soldiers who had been schooled on the Egyptian desert in biennial military exercises known as Operation Bright Star. Starting in 1980, as many as 5,000 troops at a time have maneuvered through a two-day scripted battle over harsh desert terrain. Many of the exercises were held on the barren floor of Egypt's Wadi al-Natrun, a flat, low area southeast of the Nile Delta, where the dust can be blinding and the monotonous landscape is the refuge of unfriendly creatures such as scorpions and clouds of flies.

While nature was challenging the fighting forces, military planners, lacking predeployed supplies, were rehearsing the carefully orchestrated moves that both ensure the timely arrival of hardware and troops and provide adequate amounts of water, food, and medical supplies. The planners learned that in the dusty desert air, every hour of flight time required eight hours of maintenance—roughly double the normal ratio. They discovered that they could not furnish bottled water in sufficient quantities, given the number of troops and the heat, and that well water had to be purified. They imported satellite dishes so that signal units could communicate by voice, computer, or facsimile with the United States or across the wadi to neighboring units. Providing security for U.S. personnel and bridging the language barrier offered further challenges.

The payoff came in 1990, with the successful deployment of U.S. forces to Saudi Arabia during the Persian Gulf crisis.

tions chief, forewarned by telephone that something hot was coming, ripped off the paper and scanned it. He quickly logged in what he had read and dashed out of the communications center to give it to his commander. The message in his hand would jolt the 24th into a frenzy of activity. Along with their tanks, artillery, and rocket launchers, the troops were bound for distant deserts and a potential conflict of major proportions.

Still, the order was not entirely unexpected. After 100,000 Iraqi soldiers seized Kuwait on August 2, the division had buzzed with speculation about how the president would respond. If there was action, the 24th Infantry, the Army's premier desert fighting force, would almost certainly be in the thick of it. The division had trained extensively for this role, joining Egyptian soldiers for maneuvers in Egypt every two years and conducting exercises in California's Mojave Desert, where conditions resemble those in the arid expanses of the Middle East.

On August 7, Secretary of Defense Richard Cheney had returned from Saudi Arabia, where he and that country's leaders had worked out the details that would allow the deployment of American troops on Saudi soil for the first time. The next day, President George Bush drew what he called a "line in the sand," announcing that the United States would defend Saudi Arabia in an action soon to be dubbed Operation Desert Shield. Even as the president was informing the nation, elements of the 82d Airborne, dispatched from Fort Bragg, North Carolina, were aboard C-141s making the seventeen-hour flight to the Persian Gulf. A day later, four of the MPS supply ships that had been prepositioned years earlier at Diego Garcia in the Indian Ocean were steaming toward the Gulf to meet Marines who would be flown to the scene of the crisis. And before the end of the month, the 24th Infantry and other armored forces would be in position to block Saddam Hussein's army—a response time that would amaze the world.

The 16,600 troops and support personnel of the division began a well-rehearsed deployment ritual within minutes of receiving notice of their mission from the Joint Chiefs. Processing stations popped up in dining facilities, auditoriums, and gymnasiums. Soldiers went through the lines, verifying emergency data cards that designated next of kin and indicated who was to receive their pay in the event of death. Inoculations were updated by the medics, and legal-affairs specialists helped soldiers who wanted to sign powers of attorney for use by wives and families. The soldiers showed their dog tags—small stainless-steel identification plates worn on a chain around the neck and imprinted with name, serial number, religion,

and blood type. If a tag was missing, a new one was made on the spot. Dental records were updated for identification purposes.

Lines formed at pay phones as soldiers—Company B Buzzards among them—took advantage of their last chance to call relatives. Unfamiliar terms such as *mustard gas* and *jihad* (holy war) crept into the long-distance family conversations. The soldiers knew that in a few hours they would be cut off from communications, not only because of a heavy work load but also because they might have information that could endanger the lives of those already deployed.

Among the busiest people were the supply NCOs, who had to come up with an added $50 million in vehicles, ammunition, flak jackets, uniforms, chemical-protection gear, and spare parts to fill out the division's quota of equipment and supplies. These logistics personnel were astonished when, less than twenty-four hours after they had submitted hundreds of requisitions, eighteen-wheel tractor-trailers lined up at the Fort Stewart receiving docks to drop off their loads.

To accomplish this delivery of needed matériel, technicians at Pine Bluff Arsenal, Arkansas, labored around the clock to overhaul, inspect, and test 430 M17 protective masks a day. They stepped up the pace at Redstone Arsenal, Alabama, where they readied missiles. Fifteen truckloads of ammunition per day were pulled from 902 grass-covered storage igloos at Letterkenny Army Depot in Pennsylvania. And at the Pueblo Depot in Colorado, workers, beaverlike, prepared to ship the vitally important reverse-osmosis water purification systems.

Most of the attention was focused on the division's tanks, trucks, armored personnel carriers, tracked artillery, and self-propelled rocket launchers. Each vehicle was carefully inspected; the maintenance personnel made sure it contained all the necessary ancillary equipment and documents—gas cans, tools, logs, and manuals.

When the Company B tank drivers heard their unit called, they drove their M1s to a railroad siding at Fort Stewart. There, a trained unit of the division, the railhead detachment, supervised the maneuver of the vehicles up special ramps and onto waiting flatcars. After the tanks were lashed down with chains, trains were made up, and diesel locomotives, straining to move the heavy load, headed toward the port of Savannah, forty miles away. At the docks, local stevedores off-loaded the vehicles from the rail cars and drove them up ramps and into the cavernous spaces of a fast sealift ship.

By August 13, the first FSS that would carry the equipment and supplies of the 24th Infantry to the Gulf had been loaded. Throngs of flag-waving well-wishers cheered as the great vessel moved away from the dock and headed seaward. The 24th Infantry band added a determined and uplifting flavor to the moment by playing the theme from the motion picture *Rocky.* Within a few days, as trains shuttled 24,000 tons from Fort Stewart to Savannah, other fast sealift ships would follow.

About a hundred of the division's soldiers traveled on board each of the vessels. They would unload vehicles at their destination—and, if necessary, would also defend the ship in the Persian Gulf. For

that purpose, they had brought along Stinger antiaircraft missiles and M167 six-barreled Vulcan antiaircraft guns.

Most of the soldiers had never been on a ship before. The pitching and rolling that seemed mild to the forty-two-member crew sent many of the first-time voyagers to the infirmary for a seasickness patch that medics placed behind one ear. At night, seeking escape from stuffy quarters below, troops squeezed their sleeping bags into whatever space they could find on deck.

Each soldier pulled daily maintenance duty, ensuring that all vehicles remained properly secured and unlikely to move in high seas. The troops also were required to learn basic seamanship skills, such as dogging a hatch (securing a watertight door), handling a line, and fighting shipboard fires. With the ship carrying fueled vehicles and vast stores of ammunition, the fire hazard was not to be taken lightly.

It was not fire, however, but mundane boiler trouble that caused the first real disruption of the sealift. Even before departing from Savannah, one FSS—loaded with helicopters and logistic support equipment—sprang a number of minor leaks in a boiler. The problem did not seem serious, and the ship proceeded on its way. But out in the Atlantic, the other boiler developed leaks. Finally, the ship had to be rescued by an ocean tug. That powerful vessel, one of seven operated by the Military Sealift Command, towed the huge

At top, in Savannah, Georgia, a gantry crane moves along its track, loading a naval transport from rows of trucks, tanks, and mobile offices and latrines (rear). At bottom, a hand-held scanner reads an identifying bar code tagged on all equipment. The information is fed into a computer program that determines each ship's loading sequence, based on the dimensions and weight of every item of cargo.

transport to the U.S. Naval Station at Rota, Spain. A second RO/RO ship was directed to go there, pick up the load, and deliver it to the Gulf while the first ship was towed to Gibraltar for repairs.

Transferring cargo from one fast sealift ship to another would be no small task. About 90 percent of the space in these ships is allotted to roll on/roll off cargo—vehicles that can be driven on and off via ramps. RO/RO operations are relatively quick and easy. Much slower and more complicated is the process used for cargo in the aft cargo holds and the spaces atop the holds. This cargo is lifted by the ship's cranes—an operation known as load on/load off (LO/LO). When the aft cargo is being transferred from one ship to another, the normal procedure is to move it from the first ship to the pier, then from the pier to the second ship. On this occasion, however, the commodore of the Fast Sealift Squadron, knowing how urgently the 24th Infantry's equipment was needed in the Persian Gulf, decided that the LO/LO transfer would be done in a way never attempted before: The ships would be placed side by side and the cargo would be moved directly from deck to deck. Some of the cargo-handling personnel in Rota were apprehensive, but the commodore persisted.

The decision raised manpower problems: Not enough stevedores were on hand for the complex transfer. Teams had to be assembled from all over the base. People who had been clerks the day before suddenly found themselves handling lines and rigging cargo slings.

Even for experts, this was dangerous work, since the cranes were lifting as much as fifty tons at a time. But the job was done with remarkable smoothness and speed. A normal ship-to-pier-to-ship transfer of cargo would have taken ten days. The ship-to-ship method pioneered at Rota performed the job in just four and a half days.

The first FSS, steaming at a peak speed of thirty-three knots, passed through the Strait of Gibraltar the afternoon of August 19. During the next three days, it crossed the Mediterranean and entered the Suez Canal on August 22 at 3:37 a.m. On August 27, it docked at the Persian Gulf port of Dammam in Saudi Arabia. Just fourteen days after leaving Savannah, the matériel for the lead elements of the 24th Mechanized Infantry had reached its destination—precisely on schedule.

Soldiers clad in tan desert camouflage were there waiting. Three days earlier, they had filed aboard C-5 Galaxies and C-141 Starlifters at Hunter Army Airfield, flown 8,600 miles, refueled twice in the

Marines garbed in desert camouflage pitch in to roll an Army AH-64 Apache helicopter, its rotor blades folded in shipping position, from a C-5B Galaxy transport aircraft in Saudi Arabia. Having arrived in Saudi Arabia early, the Marines were available to help prepare for the arrival of the armored forces.

air, and seventeen hours after takeoff, touched down in a Saudi airfield about fifty miles from the Kuwait border. Still jetlagged from the trip, they were slowly adjusting to the blowing, stinging sand, to midday temperatures that sometimes reached 115 degrees, and to crowded facilities and rationed supplies. The soldiers slept in a long warehouse, open at both ends to allow the air to circulate. Inside were hundreds of cots placed end to end, with a narrow walking space beside each. Latrine facilities were outdoors. Water was carefully apportioned: The troops were required to wash daily but were called up by roster for bathing only once every two to seven days. This was a long way from Georgia.

Now, energized by the arrival of the equipment, they got busy helping with the off-loading. On the last day of August, a mere three

Toward sunrise on August 27, 1990, an M1 Abrams main battle tank of the 24th Infantry Division rolls down the ramp of a fast sealift ship after a two-week journey to Saudi Arabia. The gun is pointed to the rear for shipping to reduce the space occupied by each tank.

weeks after President George Bush had ordered troops to Saudi Arabia, the rumble and clatter of American armor boomed out over the desert. Given the looming nearness of an Iraqi tank armada, the noise was welcome to all who heard it.

The Company B Buzzards were back in their tanks. Assigned to defend ports and oil refineries, they headed northward among the other troops and armor of the 24th Infantry—a fast-moving, hard-hitting team of tanks, cavalry, infantry, and artillery. Churning forward in the shimmering heat, they presented a spectacle of power guaranteed to give pause to any foe. Most impressive of all, they had materialized almost half a world away from their starting point at a speed that was a kind of logistic miracle. America's armored fist had developed lightning reflexes. ★

Realistic Training for Armored Warfare

As often as there have been wars, history has demonstrated that no amount of instruction can fully prepare combatants for the real thing. But experiencing a close simulation of battle minimizes the gap. Just this sort of harrowing tutelage is the specialty of the National Training Center at Fort Irwin, California—the premier site for combined-arms training in the United States. There, visiting mechanized infantry and armored units face a resident foe trained in Warsaw Pact tactics common among potential enemies of the United States and outfitted with up-to-date equipment.

On this particular battlefield, weapons fire laser beams, not live rounds. All of the weaponry is electronically linked to a computerized referee called a multiple integrated laser engagement system—MILES for short—which records hits and misses. With MILES, the troops can fight as if their lives depended on it without suffering real harm. As the battle proceeds, every move they make is monitored. Transmitters on their vehicles constantly signal their location, allowing technicians in an operations center at the heart of the training center to track the action in detail, collecting data the tank commanders will use later to compare what they thought happened with what actually did happen. Still more information is gathered by mobile television crews and by observer-controllers who are stationed in the field to enforce boundaries and other rules and to judge the effects of simulated mines, artillery, and chemical agents.

A review of the facts invariably leaves trainees much the wiser. But they are not the only beneficiaries. At Fort Irwin, an NTC official explained, "Tank commanders can try anything. If they win, they win. The book doesn't matter. We rewrite the book according to what we learn here."

Silhouetted in the early-morning light, tanks and armored personnel carriers belonging to Fort Irwin's resident opposition pause before moving out to engage a training unit in the Mojave Desert. Since 1981, when the National Training Center was established, these battalions have won more than 80 percent of the battles they have fought.

Americans Schooled in the Soviet Art of War

The troops fight in Soviet-style vehicles, wear bright red stars on their uniforms, and know Soviet doctrine and tactics cold. But they are American soldiers—members of the 32d Guards Motorized Rifle Regiment, the resident opposing force (known simply as OPFOR) at the National Training Center. Devoted to preparing visiting American armored units for war in the most realistic way short of actual combat, the 32d Guards take to the Mojave fourteen times a year to play the role of Warsaw Pact forces, and they make persuasive teachers.

OPFOR commanders apply tactics that are gleaned from captured Soviet manuals and updated as new tactics emerge. In keeping with the long-held Soviet philosophy of armor, they are willing to sacrifice men and matériel to seize territory, and they fre-quently order massive assaults in which the attackers outnumber the training units in manpower and armored vehicles by three to one or more. During such an assault OP-FOR often employs smoke and simulated chemical agents to heighten the shock and confusion of real war.

Even their vehicles look the part. The 32d Guards fight in American tanks and other vehicles that have been modified to look like Soviet-made T-72 tanks, BMP armored personnel carriers, self-propelled 122-mm howitzers, and ZSU-23-4 mobile antiair-craft guns. The realism impresses the train-ees. "Some of them actually think we're authentic," one OPFOR member com-plained. "Sometimes I want to walk up and show them my ID card and say that we're on the same side."

LASER SENSORS

FAKE 73-MM
GUN BARREL

TRANSMITTER
ANTENNA

FAKE SAGGER
MISSILE

MISSING
MAIN GUN

HOFFMAN
CHARGES

KILL LIGHT

LASER SENSOR

An OPFOR commander consults a map atop a Sheridan M551 tank whose main gun has been removed. A plastic Sagger missile and a small fake barrel have been added to make the vehicle resemble a Soviet BMP personnel carrier. Like all the armor used in force-on-force training, the modified Sheridan fires coded, eye-safe lasers, not live rounds, while devices called Hoffman charges mimic the flash and roar of gunfire and a transmitter automatically reports the action to the operations center. Sensors strapped to the turret's side detect incoming fire, distinguish what kind of weapon was used, and cause the kill light to flash twice after a near miss, four to six times after a hit, and steadily if the BMP has been destroyed. Similar sensors on the commander's vest and helmet would cause a buzzer to sound if he were killed.

Applying a knowledge of the terrain made keen by constant practice, an OPFOR T-72 *(in circle at left)* hides in a ravine while an attack helicopter—a UH-1H Huey fitted with a false nose and fake weapons or fake pylons to look like a Soviet Hind—scouts the area ahead.

A Sheridan altered to resemble a Soviet T-72 heads home after expending its Hoffman charges. Fiberglass panels attached to the turret and to the front of the body above the tracks give the angular Sheridan the rounded appearance of the T-72. To re-create the T-72's long 125-mm gun, a fiberglass tube has been attached to the M551's stubby cannon. Tarps covering its searchlight and .50-caliber machine gun keep the dust out.

In a tactical operations center hastily established under camouflage netting, a Blue Force commander marks maps with intelligence gathered by a scout *(solid green uniform)*. Timely reconnaissance plays an important role in how well a unit fares against OPFOR.

Well-Armed Units to Be Baptized by Laser Fire

Troops visiting the National Training Center for an education in the rigors of battle go by the name of Blue Force during their stay.

Typically, the Blue Force includes a heavy armor battalion and a mechanized infantry battalion, along with artillery, air-combat, and combat-support units from bases across the country. During their twenty-day rotation, they often fight OPFOR round the clock and endure much of the stress of actual war, such as maintaining their vehicles, providing for refueling and resupply, and tending to casualties, which are simulated. The training units are usually beaten by OPFOR, which practices more frequently than they can, but winning is not the real goal.

After each mission, the soldiers attend reviews conducted by observer-controllers—experienced NTC personnel who also serve as umpires during the fighting. All Blue Force troops review data gathered by computer as well as videotape and radio recordings, discuss what happened and why, then try again. And after their rotation, their unit commanders are given a summary of their experiences that they can consult when training back at the home base.

Planning to use combined firepower to check an OPFOR attack, a Blue Force M1 Abrams main battle tank leads three M2 Bradley infantry fighting vehicles to a defensive position. Deployed together, they present a potent threat to OPFOR's massed armor: The mobile Bradleys will concentrate on BMPs and other light armor, while the Abrams deals with the heavy T-72s of the enemy.

Opting not to use explosives, OPFOR combat engineers risk exposure to Blue Force small-arms fire to cut through a barbed-wire obstacle. Blowing open the barrier would be quicker, but the blast might give away their position.

Erecting and Overcoming Obstacles under Fire

As in a real war, OPFOR and Blue Force armored and mechanized units go to battle supported by combat engineers. Night and day, these engineers will be called on to perform three crucial missions.

The first is to hamper the mobility of the enemy. To do this, they string concertina wire, dig antitank ditches, and place simulated antitank and antipersonnel mines that seal off vital areas or channel attackers into killing zones where they can be pounded by artillery.

The second mission is to open and main-tain essential routes. Both sides have vehicles that lay bridges, plow through ditches, and shoot line charges that are capable of clearing long, wide lanes through wire and minefields. Occasionally, however, path-clearing work must be accomplished by hand *(inset above)*—perhaps under fire.

Finally, engineers help their units survive in combat by digging trenches and building berms for artillery and by excavating ingenious combat positions that permit tanks to hide unseen, then roll forward to fight, exposing only their turrets to hostile fire.

Marking a path already cleared wide enough for a tank to pass safely through, an OPFOR engineer pulls a white tape across a field littered with antipersonnel mines—simulated by blue pieces of wood—while the men behind him provide protective fire. Hoping to slow the enemy but lacking time to bury the mines, the Blue Force scattered them above the ground.

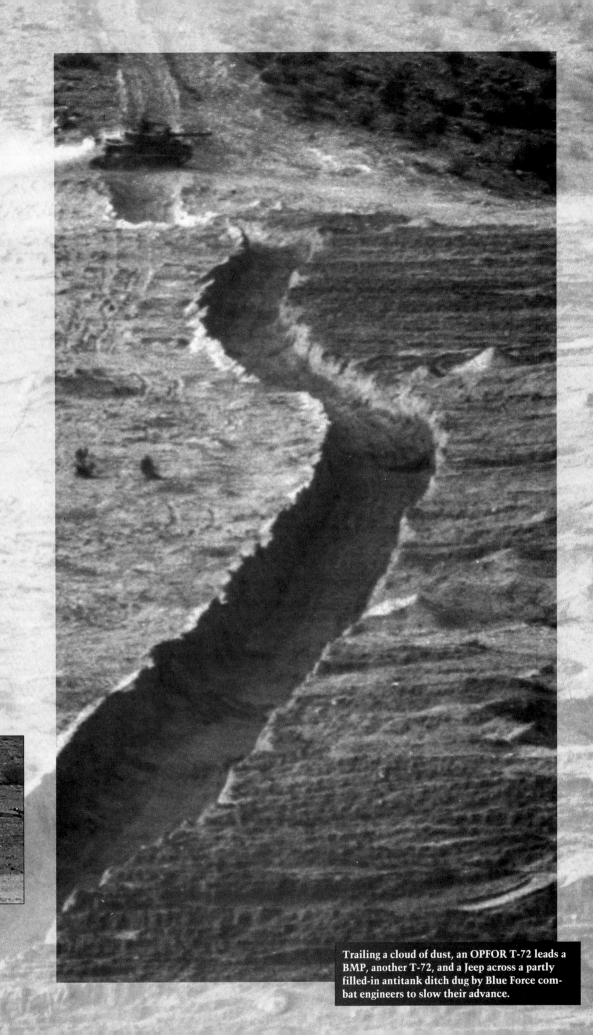

Trailing a cloud of dust, an OPFOR T-72 leads a BMP, another T-72, and a Jeep across a partly filled-in antitank ditch dug by Blue Force combat engineers to slow their advance.

Claps of Thunder from a Cloudless Desert Sky

Not all of the training that goes on at Fort Irwin takes place on the ground. Army units visiting the National Training Center typically bring their own helicopters, including OH-58 Kiowa scouts and AH-1 Cobra and AH-64 Apache gunships. The Air Force also gets into the act. Squadrons deploying from George Air Force Base, about seventy miles from Fort Irwin, provide close air support for the Blue Force in A-10 Thunderbolt IIs and contribute other aircraft for use as forward air controllers. OPFOR uses F-16s and other aircraft that make air strikes as proxy MiG-29s.

Safety considerations place some curbs on the aerial participants. Helicopters are not allowed to climb above 200 feet and planes cannot dive below 300 feet. Moreover, during force-on-force training, all aircraft are required to fly without munitions; instead, they shoot their victims with video cameras. Still, the aerial arena is anything but tame. Resident electronic-warfare specialists at Fort Irwin simulate threats from ground-based OPFOR antiaircraft missiles and radar-aimed artillery, forcing Blue Force pilots to take evasive action as they wage war from above.

After attacking OPFOR, an A-10 Thunderbolt drops a high-temperature flare while three Blue Force M1 tanks and an observer-controller vehicle, flying two flags, move forward. Such air strikes are coordinated by an air liaison officer, shown in the inset picture clutching his charts and using a radio atop an M113 armored cavalry assault vehicle. He works closely with ground commanders and serves as a conduit of strike requests to the pilots above.

A Blue Force Cobra gunship flies nap-of-the-earth—only ten to twenty feet above the rocks *(foreground)*—ahead of an unarmed OH-6 Cayuse observation helicopter. If OPFOR armor is spotted, the Cobra pilot can launch a TOW missile, blending into the rocky terrain while he guides the weapon toward the target.

The Unsung Heroes of Armored Warfare

Frequently, the real heroes at the National Training Center are not the tankers but the mechanized infantry. Riding into battle alongside tanks in the M2 Bradley infantry fighting vehicle *(below)*, mechanized infantry can significantly strengthen a Blue Force armored unit. The Bradley's 25-mm chain gun—a motorized cannon that fires up to 475 rounds per minute—can destroy lightly armored vehicles; its twin TOW missiles can kill tanks. And soldiers inside the M2 can shoot at OPFOR infantrymen through firing ports in the hull.

Infantrymen often have to leave their M2s, however, to play other roles in battle—clearing obstacles and dug-in positions, taking part in heliborne assaults, securing prisoners, and laying ambushes. Able to maneuver in all terrains and weath-er conditions, they are well suited to seizing and holding enemy territory, fighting in areas that are impassable to tanks and other vehicles, and breaching fixed obstacles.

Though exposed to small-arms fire, chemical and biological agents, artillery and mortar fire, and other dangers, the dismounted infantrymen can still be lethal to tanks. They are able to destroy targets up to 3,750 meters away with TOW missiles, those within 1,000 meters with bipod-supported missiles called Dragons, and vehicles up to 200 meters distant with shoulder-launched antitank weapons.

It is not work for the fainthearted: A soldier who has fired a wire-guided TOW or Dragon must track his target for ten to twelve seconds before impact—an eternity on the battlefield.

Noses down, UH-60A Black Hawks carrying Blue Force infantry lift off the desert floor and set out toward a predesignated landing zone. The helicopters will fly at low altitude, using the rolling sand hills and lava rock outcroppings of the Mojave Desert for concealment.

OPFOR infantrymen dash through the purple haze of a smoke grenade popped to signal the beginning of a tactical advance. Transported rapidly by infantry fighting vehicles to a place where they could dismount safely, the troops now race to their firing positions on foot.

Members of an OPFOR antitank unit fire a simulated Dragon missile from a hastily established defensive position. At the rear of the launcher, a small flash charge mimics the backblast that could give the position away in real combat.

As BMPs and T-72s advance through the early-morning gloom, a lone beacon flashes atop a tank knocked out during the early stages of an attack by the OPFOR regiment. By battle's end, amber kill lights will blanket the Mojave plain, leaving the Blue Force with a sobering lesson it can carry into its next battle—perhaps a real one.

Acknowledgments

The editors wish to thank Guy Aceto, *Air Force Magazine*, Arlington, Va.; Julius Alexander, Lockheed Aeronautical Systems, Marietta, Ga.; Sgt. Greg Allen, Ft. Carson, Colo.; Maj. Jim Bates, Military Airlift Command, Scott Air Force Base, Ill.; Lt. Col. James E. Bessler, U.S. Army, Huntsville, Ala.; Ruth Blevins, Military Traffic Management Command, Falls Church, Va.; Douglas Brown, Washington; Véronique Cardineau, Paris; Sfc. Jaime Cavazos, National Training Center, Ft. Irwin, Calif.; Jack Coffey, Forces Command, Ft. McPherson, Ga.; Sfc. Francis L. Cox, Indianapolis, Ind.; Col. Andy DeLena, Ft. McPherson; Bob DeMichele, Ft. Knox, Ky.; Lorna Dodt, Pentagon, Washington; Jack A. Duganne, McDonnell Douglas Electronic Systems, Santa Ana, Calif.; Col. Andrew S. Dulina III, Forces Command, Ft. McPherson; Lt. Gen. Charles W. Dyke, McLean, Va.; Bruce Edwards, Military Traffic Management Command; David Eshel and Tamir Eshel, Hod Hasharon, Israel; Armando E. Framarini, U.S. Army Ordnance Museum, Aberdeen Proving Ground, Md.; Mona Goss, Military Traffic Management Command; Hans Halberstadt, Very Moving Pictures, San Jose, Calif.; David Halevy, Chevy Chase Village, Md.; Richard Hallman, *Atlanta Journal & Constitution*, Atlanta, Ga.; Lt. Col. Douglas M. Harris, Ft. Carson; Sgt. Michael Harrison, Ft. Carson; Myra Hess, U.S. Army, Picatinny Arsenal, N.J.; M. Sgt. Gil High, U.S. Army Sergeants Major Academy, Ft. Bliss, Tex.; Margaret Holtz, Military Sealift Command, Washington; Hugh Howard, Pentagon; Capt. Jody Howell, Ft. Carson; David C. Isby, Alexandria, Va.; Per Jansson, AB Bofors, Bofors, Sweden; Avigdor Kahalani, Nes Ziona, Israel; Maj. Peter M. Keating, U.S. Army, Pentagon; Maj. Don Keeling, Ft. Stewart, Ga.; Gary Kieffer, Photo Press International, Alexandria, Va.; Col. David R. Kiernan, U.S. Army, Pentagon; Hal Klopper, McDonnell Douglas Helicopter Company, Mesa, Ariz.; Kermit Kramer, Alliant Techsystems, Hopkins, Minn.; Michael Lopez, *Soldiers*, Alexandria, Va.; Lt. Col. Terry McCann, Ft. Carson; Tonya McCullough, Military Sealift Command; Kenneth R. McGinty, Martin Marietta Electronics Systems, Orlando, Fla.; Christine MacKinnon, Military Sealift Command; Charles P. Manor III, Martin Marietta, Bethesda, Md.; Eric Micheletti, "Histoire et Collections", Paris; Gary R. Milam, U.S. Army Armor School, Ft. Knox; Susan Miles, Lockheed Aeronautical Systems, Marietta, Ga.; Irene Miner, Pentagon; Lyle Minter, Pentagon; Frank Misurelli, U.S. Army, Picatinny Arsenal; Felix Müller, Oerlikon-Contraves, Zurich; Lt. Col. David W. Owen (Ret.), CRC Systems, Inc., Böblingen, Germany; Capt. Larry Padron, Ft. Carson; Sylvie Papillon, Direction Générale de l'Armement, Paris; Mary Ponthan, St. Louis Park, Minn.; Debbie Reed, Pentagon; Peter J. Rowland, U.S. Army, Picatinny Arsenal; Burno Roy, Direction Générale de l'Armement, Paris; David Rubinger, Jerusalem; Maj. Gen. Ibrahim Shakeeb (Ret.), Cairo; Mike Sierra, ITTA, Washington; Maj. Karel Sigtenhorst, U.S. Army Armor School, Ft. Knox; Lt. Col. Edward P. Stafford, Jr., Ft. McPherson; Dennis Steele, *Army*, Arlington, Va.; Bill Steinbicker, Alliant Techsystems, Minnetonka, Minn.; Maj. Donald Stevenson, U.S. Army Armor School, Ft. Knox; Greg Stewart, Laguna Beach, Calif.; 1st Sgt. Edward Sunowski, Ft. Knox; Mabel Thomas, Pentagon; S. Sgt. Gordon Tom, Sacramento, Calif.; Laurie Viggiano, Ft. Knox; Art Volpe, U.S. Army Tank Automotive Command, Warren, Mich.; Maj. John Wagstaffe, National Training Center, Ft. Irwin; Lt. Col. Scott Wallace, National Training Center, Ft. Irwin; Capt. Jeffrey Weber, U.S. Army Armor School, Ft. Knox; George C. Wilson, Washington; Steven Zaloga, Stamford, Conn.; Ahmad Ziada, Dar al-Hilal Library, Cairo.

Bibliography

BOOKS

Adan, Avraham (Bren), *On the Banks of the Suez.* Novato, Calif.: Presidio Press, 1980.

el Badri, Hassan, Taha el Magdoub, and Mohammed Dia el Din Zohdy, *The Ramadan War, 1973.* Dunn Loring, Va.: T. N. Dupuy Associates, 1978.

Barnaby, Frank, *The Automated Battlefield.* New York: Macmillan, 1986.

Cordier, Sherwood S., *U.S. Military Power and Rapid Deployment Requirements in the 1980s.* Boulder, Colo.: Westview Press, 1983.

Dartford, Mark, ed., *Military Technology.* New York: Simon & Schuster, 1985.

Dayan, Moshe, *Moshe Dayan: Story of My Life.* New York: Warner Books, 1976.

Doleman, Edgar C., Jr., and the Editors of Boston Publishing Company, *Tools of War* (The Vietnam Experience series). Boston, Mass.: Boston Publishing, 1985.

Dupuy, Col. Trevor N., *Elusive Victory.* New York: Harper & Row, 1978.

Eshel, David, *Chariots of the Desert.* Washington: Brassey's Defence Publishers, 1989.

Foss, Christopher F., *Jane's AFV Recognition Handbook.* New York: Jane's Publishing, 1987.

Geddes, J. Philip, *Apache.* Alexandria, Va.: International Defense Images, no date.

Goad, K. J. W., and D. H. J. Halsey, *Ammunition (In-cluding Grenades and Mines).* Volume 3 of *Brassey's Battlefield Weapons Systems and Technology.* Elmsford, N.Y.: Pergamon Press, 1982.

Guderian, Gen. Heinz, *Panzer Leader.* Transl. by Constantine Fitzgibbon. New York: Dutton, 1952.

Gunston, Bill, and Mike Spick, *Modern Fighting Helicopters.* New York: Crescent Books, 1986.

Halberstadt, Hans:
  Army Aviation. Novato, Calif.: Presidio Press, 1990.
  NTC: A Primer of Modern Land Combat. Novato, Calif.: Presidio Press, 1989.

Herzog, Maj. Gen. Chaim, *The War of Atonement.* Boston: Little, Brown, 1975.

Hilmes, Rolf, *Main Battle Tanks: Developments in Design since 1945.* Transl. by Richard Simpkin. Washington: Brassey's Defence Publishers, 1987.

Hunnicutt, R. P., *Abrams: A History of the American Main Battle Tank.* Volume 2. Novato, Calif.: Presidio Press, 1990.

The Insight Team of the London *Sunday Times, The Yom Kippur War.* New York: Doubleday,1974.

Isby, David C., *Weapons and Tactics of the Soviet Army.* New York: Jane's Publishing, 1988.

Jane's Aircraft Spectacular: Hercules. Ed. by Mike Gaines. New York: Jane's Publishing, 1984.

Jane's All the World's Aircraft 1987-88. Ed. by John

W. R. Taylor. New York: Jane's Publishing, 1987.

Jane's Armour and Artillery 1988-89. New York: Jane's Publishing, 1989.

Jane's Weapon Systems 1988-89. Ed. by Bernard Blake. New York: Jane's Publishing, 1988.

Kahalani, Avigdor, *The Heights of Courage.* Westport, Conn.: Greenwood Press, 1984.

Kelly, Orr, *King of the Killing Zone.* New York: W. W. Norton, 1989.

Macksey, Kenneth:
   Guderian: Creator of the Blitzkrieg. New York: Stein and Day, 1976.
   Tank versus Tank. Topsfield, Mass.: Salem House, 1988.

The Military Balance 1989-1990. London: The International Institute for Strategic Studies, 1989.

Miller, David, and Christopher F. Foss, *Modern Land Combat.* New York: Portland House, 1987.

Perrett, Bryan, *Knights of the Black Cross.* New York: St. Martin's Press, 1986.

Quarrie, Bruce, and Mike Spick, *An Illustrated Guide to Tank Busters.* New York: Prentice Hall, 1987.

Seitelman, Mi, ed., *Advanced Combat Helicopters.* Osceola, Wis.: Motorbooks International, 1988.

Starry, Gen. Donn A., *Armored Combat in Vietnam.* Salem, N.H.: The Ayer Company, 1982.

Stevens, Lawrence, *Laser Basics.* Englewood Cliffs, N.J.: Prentice-Hall, 1985.

Tanks Illustrated 8: U.S. Battle Tanks Today. Harrisburg, Pa.: Arms and Armour Press, 1984.

Taylor, Michael, *Encyclopedia of Modern Military Aircraft.* New York: W. H. Smith, 1987.

The World's Great Military Helicopters. New York: W. H. Smith, 1990.

Zaloga, Steven J., *The M1 Abrams Battle Tank.* London: Osprey Publishing, 1985.

Zaloga, Steven J., and Lt. Col. James W. Loop, *Modern American Armor.* Harrisburg, Pa.: Arms and Armour Press, 1982.

PERIODICALS

Adams, James, "Tank Dogged by Disappointment." London *Sunday Times,* Sept. 16, 1990.

Adams, Peter, "Red Army Digest: Lessons from Afghanistan." *Army Times,* Apr. 23, 1990.

Allen, Scott, "Soldiers at Sea." *Soldier,* Nov. 1990.

"Armored Gun System to Give Light Units Antiarmor Punch." *Army,* July 1987.

Atkinson, Rick, and George C. Wilson, "Land War: Centerpiece of Strategy." *Washington Post,* Dec. 8, 1990.

"The Balance of Forces in the Gulf: In the Region and En Route." *Washington Post,* Aug. 15, 1990.

Beck, Melinda, et al., "Fighting in the Desert." *Newsweek,* Aug. 27, 1990.

Berge, Sven, "Design Concept of the S-Tank." *Armada International Special,* Jan. 1983.

Born in Battle (Israel), Issue 3, Oct. 6, 1973.

Bowden, Capt. James A., "The RDJTF and Doctrine." *U.S. Naval Institute Proceedings,* Nov. 1982.

Browne, Malcolm W., "America's Mightiest Tank." *Discover,* June 1982.

Budiansky, Stephen, "The Failure to Match Weapons with Words." *U.S. News & World Report,* Sept. 24, 1990.

Burniece, Joseph R., and Paul A. Hoven, "T-62, T-64, T-72, T-80, T-?: Understanding Soviet MBT Development." *Military Technology,* May 1984.

Bussert, Jim, "Is the RDF a Rapid Deployment Farce?" *Military Electronics/Countermeasures,* Apr. 1982.

"Chief among Indians," *Flight International* (England), Oct. 15, 1988.

Christy, John, "M-1 Abrams: The Army's New Main Battle Tank Is America's Front Line Armored Fist!" *International Combat Arms,* Jan. 1985.

Correll, John T., "The Power-Projection Shortfall." *Air Force Magazine,* Aug. 1988.

Cushman, John H., Jr., "Inside the Arsenals." *New York Times Magazine,* Sept. 16, 1990.

Davis, R. Louis, "Resupply Operations Continue: MTMC Morale Remains High in Spite of Increased Workload." *The Military Traffic Management Command Expediter* (U.S. Army), Oct. 1990.

DeParle, Jason, "Despair, Calm and Disdain Greet Mobilization at Bragg." *Washington Post,* Aug. 13, 1990.

"Deployment: The Army's Response." *Soldiers,* Oct. 1990.

"The Desert Devils." *Soldiers,* Feb. 1986.

"Desert Shield: Our Line in the Sand." *Army,* Oct. 1990.

Evans, David, "Army Caught Short on Tank Supply Lines." *Chicago Tribune,* Sept. 12, 1990.

Ewing, Lee, "24th Division is Ready in the Desert." *Fairfax Journal* (Virginia), Sept. 7, 1990.

"The Forces Build Up." *Time,* Aug. 27, 1990.

Fulghum, David A., "U.S. Airlift to Mideast Is Biggest Ever Mounted." *Aviation Week & Space Technology,* Aug. 20, 1990.

Gilleland, Donald L., "M1A2: The Evolution Continues." *Defence* (Surrey, England), Oct. 1989.

Goodman, Glenn W., Jr., "Joint Hypervelocity Missile Tests Near: Potential Low-Cost Tank-Killer of 1990s." *Armed Forces Journal International,* Sept. 1987.

Gordon, Michael R., "U.S. Gulf Force Steadily Builds Power to Attack." *New York Times,* Sept. 16, 1990.

Grossman, Larry, "Slow Going for Fast Sealift." *Military Forum,* Mar. 1989.

Grove, E. J., "The Shape of Tanks to Come." *NATO's Fifteen Nations,* Feb.-Mar. 1977.

Guidry, Vernon A., Jr., "(Very) Fast Ships." *Military Logistics Forum,* May 1985.

Hammick, Murray, and Christopher F. Foss, "Four Means to an End: The British Chieftain Replacement Program." *International Defense Review,* Sept. 1990.

Hammond, Jack, "Carl Gustav Recoilless Gun." *International Combat Arms,* May 1987.

Hellman, Peter, "Israel's Chariot of Fire." *The Atlantic,* Mar. 1985.

Herzberg, Robert, "Supertank: The M1 Abrams Is a Shining Example of How to Do Things Right." *International Combat Arms,* Nov. 1987.

High, Gil, "On Saudi Soil." *Soldiers,* Nov. 1990.

Homan, Arthur Lee, et al., " 'Not without Honor': An Account of the Life and Times of John Walter Christie." *Antique Automobile,* July-Aug. 1965.

"Improved Chieftain for Iran." *International Defense Review,* Apr. 1976.

Jehl, Douglas, "U.S. Military Facing Terror of Chemical War." *Los Angeles Times,* Aug. 9, 1990.

Johnson, Maj. Maxwell O., "The Role of Maritime Based Strategy." *Marine Corps Gazette,* Feb. 1984.

Johnson, Quinn, "Ultimate War Game." *High Technology,* Oct. 1986.

Kibler, Joan F., "Phase Out in Saudi Arabia." *The Military Engineer,* Mar.-Apr. 1989.

Krapke, Paul-Werner, "Battle-Tanks: Makes a Third Generation?" *Armada International,* May 1989.

Lenorovitz, Jeffrey M., "Saudi Support Contributes to Successful First Phase of Desert Shield Operation." *Aviation Week & Space Technology,* Sept. 10, 1990.

"Lockheed's Stretched Starlifter." *Air International*, Mar. 1983.

"M1 Tank." *Military Logistics Forum*, Nov./Dec. 1986.

"Maritime Prepositioning Operations." *The Military Engineer*, Mar.-Apr. 1988.

Mark, Michael E., "Force on Force." *Military*, Jan. 1990.

Martz, Ron, "GIs Confident They'll Outrun, Outgun Iraqis." *Atlanta Journal & Constitution*, Nov. 4, 1990.

Mayfield, Mark, "Thousands 'On Alert' Get Ready to Go." *USA Today*, Aug. 14, 1990.

Miles, Donna, "Filling the Pipeline." *Soldiers*, Nov. 1990.

"Military Technology Profile: M1A1 Abrams—The Winner." *Military Technology*, Oct. 1988.

"Military Technology Profile: M1A2 Abrams Characteristics." *Military Technology*, Oct. 1988.

Moore, Molly:
"Arabs Agree on Force to Defend Saudis: U.S. Deployment May Reach More than 200,000 Troops." *Washington Post*, Aug. 11, 1990.
"Crisis Pits High-Tech against Battle-Tough: Military Leaders Assess Threat Iraq's Numbers Pose to Sophisticated U.S.-Led Force." *Washington Post*, Sept. 24, 1990.
"U.S. Training, Tactics Shift with Desert Sand: Gulf Troops Adapt to Unexpected Battlefield." *Washington Post*, Nov. 25, 1990.

Morganthau, Tom, "And Now: The War of the Future." *Newsweek*, Aug. 13, 1990.

Naylor, Sean D.:
"Best Tank in the World, Some Say." *Army Times*, Oct. 8, 1990.
"Heavy Going in the Rush to the Gulf." *Army Times*, Sept. 10, 1990.

Nelan, Bruce W., "Planes against Brawn." *Time*, Aug. 20, 1990.

Nordeen, Lon O., Jr., "The Bradley under Attack: A Combined Arms Performer Endures Its Purgatory Alone." *Army*, July 1987.

Ogorkiewicz, Richard, "BILL—The Shape of Missiles to Come?" *Jane's Defence Weekly*, Dec. 13, 1986.

Patrick, Stephen B., "Tank! A Weapon System Survey." *Strategy & Tactics*, May/June 1974.

Powers, John Carr, "Tanks for the Memories." *International Combat Arms*, Jan. 1987.

Poyer, Joe, "Super Battle Tanks." *International Combat Arms*, Nov. 1988.

Prina, L. Edgar, "Two if by Sea, Are We Ready?" *Army*, Dec. 1990.

Ramo, Joshua Cooper, "Roots of Desert Operation Go Back to 1979." *Boston Globe*, Aug. 16, 1990.

"Rapid Deployment: General P. X. Kelley Reflects." *Defense & Foreign Affairs*, May 1988.

Record, Jeffrey, "The U.S. Central Command: Toward What Purpose?" *Strategic Review*, spring 1986.

Reed, Fred, "Technology Injects Realism into Tank Training." *Federal Computer Week*, Dec. 12, 1988.

Rhodes, Jeffrey P., "All Together at Fort Irwin." *Air Force*, Dec. 1989.

Scarborough, Rowan, "Deployment of 2,720 Tanks to Give U.S. an Offensive Look." *Washington Times*, Nov. 16, 1990.

Schemmer, Benjamin F., "Airlift, Sealift in Short Supply at Very Time Need Grows Fastest." *Armed Forces Journal International*, May 1989.

Schmitt, Eric:
"Pentagon Faces Daunting Challenge in Rushing Sizable Force to Mideast." *New York Times*, Aug. 14, 1990.

"Planning at the Helm for Troops in the Sand." *New York Times*, Aug. 23, 1990.

Silverberg, David, "M1A2: Saudis Will Have It, but Will Americans?" *Army Times*, Oct. 8, 1990.

Smoler, Fredric, "What Does History Have to Say about the Persian Gulf?" *American Heritage*, Nov. 1990.

Stewart, Maj. Richard A., "Ships That Can Deliver." *U.S. Naval Institute Proceedings*, Nov. 1984.

Thomas, Evan, "Special Report." *Newsweek*, Sept. 3, 1990.

"Troops." *Current News Early Bird* (Pentagon), Aug. 8, 1990.

Tucker, Anthony R., "Armoured Warfare in the Gulf." *Armed Forces*, May 1988.

Vered, G. R., "Evolution of BLAZER Reactive Armour and its Adaptation to AFVs." *Military Technology*, Dec. 1987.

Vinch, Chuck, "Experts Worry over C-141 Wing Cracks." *Pacific Stars and Stripes*, Aug. 24, 1990.

Watson, Russell:
"Drawing the Line." *Newsweek*, Aug. 20, 1990.
"Reign of Terror." *Newsweek*, June 19, 1989.

Watson, Russell, et al., "Battle Ready." *Newsweek*, Aug. 20, 1990.

Webster, Lt. J. M., Jr., "The Real Thing." *Military Traffic Management Command Expediter* (U.S. Army), Oct. 1990.

Wells, Mike, "Maritime Pre-Positioning—A New Dimension for Rapid Deployment." *Armed Forces*, Mar. 1988.

" 'What I Saw Is Bodies, Bodies, Bodies.' " *Newsweek*, June 19, 1989.

Wootten, James, *Rapid Deployment Forces*. Washington: Library of Congress Congressional Research Service, Mar. 4, 1980.

Zeybel, Lt. Col. Henry, "M1 Tank Turbine Engine Is Thirsty, but Reliable." *Army*, July 1987.

OTHER SOURCES

"Aerojet SADARM: Sense and Destroy Armor." Brochure. Azusa, Calif.: GenCorp, Aerojet Electronic Systems Division.

"Agusta A129: Integrated Helmet and Display Sighting System." Study Guide. Minneapolis, Minn.: Honeywell Corp.

"AH-64 Apache Attack Helicopter." Brochure. Mesa, Ariz.: McDonnell Douglas.

"AH-64A Apache Anti-Armor Helicopter System Description." Brochure. Mesa, Ariz.: McDonnell Douglas, Jan. 1988.

Apache Newsletter. Pamphlet. Mesa, Ariz.: McDonnell Douglas Helicopter Company, Oct. 1990.

"C-5A Galaxy." Press release. Marietta, Ga.: Lockheed Aeronautical Systems Company.

"C-141 Starlifter." Press release. Marietta, Ga.: Lockheed Aeronautical Systems Company, 1990.

"Extending the Senses." Minneapolis, Minn.: Northwest Teleproductions, June 17, 1988. Videotape.

"Hellfire: Here Today—Ready for Tomorrow." Duluth, Ga.: Rockwell International (Missile Systems Division). Videotape.

"Hellfire: Modular Weapon System." Brochure. Duluth, Ga.: Missile Systems Division, Aug. 1988.

"History and Role of Armor." Brochure. Fort Knox, Ky.: U.S. Army Armor School.

"IHADSS: Integrated Helmet and Display Sighting System." Brochure. Minneapolis, Minn.: Honeywell Corp. (Avionics Division), May 26, 1982.

"Introduction to Honeywell Helmet Sight Systems Including Applications Data and Experience." Minneapolis, Minn.: Honeywell Corp. (Avionics Division), Apr. 7, 1977.

"KE Tactical Cartridge." Brochure. St. Petersburg,

Fla.: Olin Corp., 1989.

"KIOWA Warrior: Meeting the Threat." Santa Ana, Calif.: Audio Visual Services (McDonnell Douglas Electronic Systems). Videotape.

"Libyan Military Forces Retreat from Chad." *Facts On File*, Mar. 27, 1987.

"MDHC 85-164: AH-64A Apache Anti-Armor Helicopter System Description." Brochure. Mesa, Ariz.: McDonnell Douglas Helicopter Company, Jan. 4, 1991.

"MILES: The Ultimate in Training." Brochure. Arlington, Va.: Loral Electro-Optical Systems, Oct. 1986.

"National Training Center." Brochure. Fort Irwin, Calif.

"The 105-mm APFSDS CMC105." Brochure. Waterloo, Iowa: Chamberlain Manufacturing Corporation.

"Rapid Deployment Force." Brochure. Arlington, Va.: Carroll Publishing Co., 1980.

"TADS/PNVS." Brochure. Orlando, Fla.: Martin Marietta Electronic Systems, 1990.

TADS/PNVS. Orlando, Fla.: Martin Marietta Electronic Systems, Feb. 1989. Videotape.

"TADS/PNVS with OIP." Booklet. Orlando, Fla.: Martin Marietta Electronic Systems, 1989.

"Tank, Combat, Full-Tracked: 120-mm Gun, M1A1 (2350-01-087-1095) General Abrams." Technical Manual. Washington: Headquarters, Department of the Army, Dec. 30, 1985.

"Target Acquisition Designation Sight/Pilot Night Vision Sensor." Fact Sheet. Orlando, Fla.: Martin Marietta Electronic Systems, June 1990.

"U.S. Army Missile Command Hellfire Project Office." Booklet. Redstone Arsenal, Ala., Aug. 1990.

Index

Picture Credits

The sources for the illustrations in this book are listed below. Credits from left to right are separated by semicolons, from top to bottom by dashes.
Cover: J. Pavlovsky/SYGMA. 6, 7: Co Rentmeester for LIFE. 8, 9: David Eshel, Jerusalem. 10, 11: AP/Wide World Photos. 12, 13: William Stevens/Gamma Liaison; Luc Delahaye/Sipa Press. 14, 15: Stuart Franklin/Magnum. 16: P. Durand/SYGMA. 20: Bild-archiv Preussischer Kulturbesitz, Berlin. 22: Courtesy Eshel-Dramit Ltd., Jerusalem. 25: Map by Mapping Specialists Ltd. and Susan Sanford. 26, 27: Al Hilal/Camera Press, London. 28: London *Sunday Times* (4). 30-32: Art by Lloyd K. Townsend. 34, 35: Tony McGrath/Camera Press, London. 37: Map by Mapping Specialists Ltd. and Susan Sanford. 39: Art by Fred Holz. 40, 41: Uzi Keren, courtesy Military (IDF) & Defense Establishment Archives, Israel. 42, 43: Werner Braun/Camera Press, London. 46, 47: Camera Press, London, inset Michel Laurent/Gamma Liaison. 50, 51: Courtesy Israel Government Press Office. 55: Courtesy Eshel-Dramit Ltd., Jerusalem. 58, 59: Courtesy Giora Lev, Israel. 60: Keystone, Paris. 61: David Rubinger, Jerusalem. 62, 63: Bruno Barbey/Magnum. 64, 65: Dynamit Nobel, Wehrtechnik, Troisdorf. 66, 67: Art by Mark Robinson. 68, 69: Jebb Harris/ Visions Photos Inc., insets Alliant Techsystems and art by Mark Robinson. 70: Tamir Eshel, Jerusalem; Chamberlain Manufacturing Corporation. 71: Art by Mark Robinson—courtesy Israeli Military Industries. 72, 73: AB Bofors, Bofors, Sweden (2); art by Mark Robinson (2). 74: Art by Mark Robinson—Oerlikon-Contraves Pyrotech Division, Switzerland. 75: Art by Mark Robinson—Tamir Eshel, Jerusalem. 76: Co Rentmeester/The Image Bank. 79: AP/Wide World Photos. 83: General Dynamics Land Systems. 84, 85: Art by Dale Gustafsen. 88: Ofir Karni/International Defence Forces, Israel—courtesy Eshel-Dramit Ltd., Jerusalem. 90: Nathan Albert/Bamahane—The Tank Museum, Wareham, Dorset—U.S. Army. 91: Renk AG, Augsburg—Witt/Sipa Press—Yves Debay, Paris. 93: Witt/Sipa Press. 94, 95: The Defense Matériel Administration of Sweden, Stockholm. 96-100: Hans Halberstadt/Arms Communications. 103: Art by Matt McMullen. 104: Nikolai Malyshev/SOVFOTO. 106: Hans Halberstadt/Arms Communications. 107: Greg Stewart/Arms Communications. 108, 109: Mi Seitelman/Foto Consortium; Cradle of Aviation Museum, Nassau County, N.Y. 112, 113: U.S. Army—art by Matt McMullen. 114, 115: Frederick Sutter. 116, 117: George Hall/Check

Six. 118, 119: Hans Halberstadt/Arms Communications (2)—art by Will Williams of Stansbury, Ronsaville & Wood, Inc., inset art by Jack Pardue. 120, 121: Rockwell International Corporation—art by Will Williams of Stansbury, Ronsaville & Wood, Inc. (2). 122, 123: Art by Will Williams of Stansbury, Ronsaville & Wood, Inc. 124: Military Traffic Management Command, Falls Church, Va. 127: Map by Mapping Specialists, Ltd. 128: U.S. Army. 132, 133: Lockheed Corporation. 134, 135: Mark Meyer. 139: U.S. Navy. 141: Ben-Ami Cohen, courtesy Achidatex, Jerusalem. 142, 143: M. El-Koussy/SYGMA. 144, 145: Dennis Brack/Black Star. 147: Joseph Trotz—Military Traffic Management Command, Falls Church, Va. 149: AP/Wide World Photos. 150, 151: Dennis Brack/ Black Star. 152, 153: Charlie Cole/Picture Group. 154, 155: Guy Aceto/*Air Force Magazine*, inset Hans Halberstadt/Arms Communications. 156, 157: Greg Stewart/Arms Communications. 158, 159: Greg Stewart/Arms Communications, inset Hans Halberstadt/Arms Communications. 160, 161: Greg Stewart/Arms Communications, inset Hans Halberstadt/Arms Communications. 162, 163: Greg Stewart/Arms Communications, inset Guy Aceto/ *Air Force Magazine*. 164, 165: Hans Halberstadt/ Arms Communications. 166, 167: Greg Stewart/ Arms Communications; Frank Cox/*Soldiers* magazine—Greg Stewart/Arms Communications— Frank Cox/*Soldiers* magazine. 168, 169: Guy Aceto/ *Air Force Magazine*.

Time-Life Books
is a division of Time Life Inc.,
a wholly owned subsidiary of
THE TIME INC. BOOK COMPANY

TIME-LIFE BOOKS

MANAGING EDITOR: Thomas H. Flaherty
Director of Editorial Resources: Elise D. Ritter-Clough
Director of Photography and Research:
John Conrad Weiser
Editorial Board: Dale M. Brown, Roberta Conlan, Laura Foreman, Lee Hassig, Jim Hicks, Blaine Marshall, Rita Thievon Mullin, Henry Woodhead

PUBLISHER: Joseph J. Ward

Associate Publisher: Anne Mirabito
Editorial Director: Russell B. Adams, Jr.
Marketing Director: Anne Everhart
Director of Design: Louis Klein
Production Manager: Prudence G. Harris
Supervisor of Quality Control: James King

Editorial Operations
Production: Celia Beattie
Library: Louise D. Forstall
Computer Composition: Deborah G. Tait (Manager), Monika D. Thayer, Janet Barnes Syring, Lillian Daniels

Correspondents: Elisabeth Kraemer-Singh (Bonn); Christine Hinze (London); Christina Lieberman (New York); Maria Vincenza Aloisi (Paris); Ann Natanson (Rome). Valuable assistance was also provided by Nihal Tamraz (Cairo), Otto Gobius and Robert Kroon (Geneva), Marlin Levin and Jean Max (Jerusalem), Elizabeth Brown and Katheryn White (New York), Ann Wise (Rome), Mary Johnson (Stockholm), Mieko Ikeda (Tokyo).

THE NEW FACE OF WAR

SERIES EDITOR: Lee Hassig
Series Administrator: Judith W. Shanks
Art Director: Christopher M. Register

Editorial Staff for *The Armored Fist*
Picture Editor: Marion Ferguson Briggs
Text Editors: Charlotte Anker, Paul Mathless
Assistant Editors/Researchers: Ruth Goldberg, Mark Lazen, Jennifer L. Pearce, Mark Rogers
Assistant Art Director: Fatima Taylor
Writers: Charles J. Hagner, James M. Lynch
Copy Coordinators: Elizabeth Graham (principal), Anthony K. Pordes
Editorial Assistant: Kathleen S. Walton
Picture Coordinators: Barry Anthony, David Beard

Special Contributors: Champ Clark, George Constable, George Daniels, Jerry Korn, Mark Morrow, Rod Paschall, Craig Roberts, Edward Stafford, Diane Ullius (text); John Davidson, Ellen Gross, Catherine A. Halesky, John Leigh, Barbara Jones Smith, Susan Sonnesyn, Joann Stern, Marie Tessier, Kathy Wismar, Suzanne Zima (research); Sue Ellen Pratt, Tyrone Taylor (art); Mel Ingber (index).

Library of Congress Cataloging in
Publication Data
The Armored fist/by the editors of
Time-Life Books.
    p. cm. (The New face of war series).
    Includes bibliographical references and index.
    ISBN 0-8094-8608-3
    1. Tank warfare.
I. Time-Life Books. II. Series.
UG446.5.A685 1991
358.1'8—dc20   90-21081 CIP
ISBN 0-8094-8609-1 (lib. bdg.)